D1381501

Bigger Ideas

from

Color Me Beautiful

Bigger Ideas

from

Color Me Beautiful

Colour and Style Ideas for the Fuller Figure

Mary Spillane

BCA

LONDON   NEW YORK   SYDNEY   TORONTO

*This book is dedicated to Veronique Henderson who
is Color Me Beautiful's own in-house inspiration on style.*

© 1995 Mary Spillane

Designed by Paul Saunders
Illustrations by David Downton
Author photograph on back flap of jacket by Sue Hume
Evans photographs, including cover, reproduced courtesy of Evans,
Hammond & Hughes and Ford Models
Other photography by Mike Prior

This edition published 1995
by BCA by arrangement with
Judy Piatkus (Publishers) Ltd

CN 4458

Printed in Great Britain

CONTENTS

CONVERTING INTERNATIONAL SIZES

UK	France	Germany	Italy	USA/Canada
14	42	40	44	10/12
16	44	42	46	12/14
18	46	44	48	14/16
20	48	46	50	16/18
22	50	48	52	18/20
24	52	50	54	20/22
26	54	52	56	22/24

NB Sizes in **Australia** and **New Zealand** are the same as in the UK.

ACKNOWLEDGEMENTS

This book has been a real team effort among the CMB staff and consultants, along with retailers and manufacturers.

The UK's most prominent retailer for the larger woman, Evans, offered advice and support at every stage – especially by providing photos from their own wonderful collections. Andy King, MD of Evans, and advertiser Steven Sharp deserve special thanks.

Janice Bhend, Editor of Yes! magazine and champion of the larger woman, is credited with being inspirational to our cause which has been her own for over 20 years. Dara O'Malley of J D Williams/Classic Collection readily turned over all their research on sizing which transformed their ranges to be more comfortable on today's women, regardless of size. Diane Williams and colleagues at Marks & Spencer were very helpful about underwear for the fuller figure.

Evans, Marks & Spencer, Elisabeth by Liz Claiborne, Sixteen 47, Marina Rinaldi, Jacques Vert Plus and Adrian Mann all provided fashions for the specially commissioned photography by Mike Prior. David Downton supplied stunning artwork.

Veronique Henderson is credited with sorting out the rainbow of colour tints and coordinating the fashions for the photo sessions. When we had a gap, she readily raided her own wardrobe for the right piece. Muriel Brightmore patiently draped the tailor's dummies (pages 100-110). And what aspirational models: Sarah Forbes, Sally Ely, Natasha Osuna and Karen Mason, and Pippa and Alison of Hammond Hughes, are all gorgeous examples of bigger, beautiful women.

Mike Prior took wonderful photographs, Martyn Fletcher looked after hair and make-up, and designer Paul Saunders made sure everything looked good on the page.

Anna and Lucy Luscombe were particularly long-suffering and helpful to mum, sorting and selecting photos over weekends.

Judy Piatkus and Gill Cormode at Piatkus Books supported the concept of this special guide from conception and have done everything to make it our best endeavour yet. Sue Fleming skilfully cut my prose down to size after Sue Abbott, my PA for over a decade, proofed it up for the umpteenth time. Working quietly but persistently has been Heather Rocklin, who made sure it all came together on time.

INTRODUCTION

This book is about possibilities. It is a style guide for a growing number of women who aren't served as well as they should be, with clothes and images that they want, by either the high street shops or the fashion media. These are the large, healthy, attractive women of size 16 and over (12/14 and over in the USA and Canada), who know they can look wonderful, but are frustrated by the lack of similar options in colour, style and price to those offered to smaller women. Neither do they get the full range of advice and tips from the experts about how to look their best.

For over ten years, the Color Me Beautiful organisation has written books and offered help to all women on every aspect of their images. But we've become increasingly aware from our readers and clients, and from our own larger consultants, that bigger women only benefit from a *portion* of the style advice available. So, the time has come for a complete style guide focussed on *your* bodies and *your* possibilities.

I can't argue that being big automatically means being beautiful any more than anyone can assert that simply being a small size makes one beautiful. Looking terrific takes some know-how and some work for all women. The key to looking your best is learning how to dress *your* best. When you flatter what you've got, you can look wonderful. Every big woman can be beautiful when she learns how to make the most of *her* natural beauty.

The Feel-good Factor

OPPOSITE **Party Time**
If you've got it, then show it! Flirty little dresses should swing never cling…

Some women feel so rotten about themselves, however, that no matter how well they dress, they still can't look beautiful. This can be a problem for women of any size. You have got to begin from the premise that you

...But if you are less confident about showing your limbs, wrap them up in something huggable .

are worth bothering about. Make a good start in believing that you are worth some thought and attention just by reading this book!

It's not that you and every bigger woman do not have plenty of wonderful features to work with – all women of every size have assets to be proud of. But if you can't *feel* optimistic about yourself and your possibilities as a person, you will always project a lacklustre and inferior image, an image that falls far short of your true potential beauty.

You Are Big News!

In the past few years, Color Me Beautiful has been asked increasingly by TV programmes and magazines to do makeovers on bigger women. It's become all the rage, mainly because retailers seem to be waking up to the fact that there is a huge market (no pun intended) of consumers not spending as much as they would like. What an opportunity, they now recognise. So, everyone is tripping over themselves to serve you.

Makeovers for anyone over a size 14 (10/12 USA/Canada) were a nightmare not so long ago. We would have to scour the manufacturers for the right options, only to be forced to compromise on colour and shape due to the lack of availability. It was so frustrating to work with women keen to improve their image, but who had little hope of finding the clothes to do the job. But as you will see in the wonderful photographs we've used in this book, and in the directory at the back, your fashions are now big business. At every price point – on the high street, via mail order or even TV home shopping – you can select wonderful fashions to suit you.

Our Role Models

At CMB Image Consultants we have been recruiting consultants who are average in size and looks – but never in potential! – since we began in 1983. We don't discriminate against any size, but do our best to find dynamo beauticians, stylists and trainers who want to become image consultants. If they are larger, then so much the better, as many of our clients are also large. We now have a team of beautiful women and men

– young, mid-life and older – who look fabulous in their right colours and best styles. The women range from the small sizes through to sizes 16 to 22 (12/14 to 18/20 in US/Canadian sizes).

CMB consultants are walking testaments to our principles. Once you know how to play the game, you can fool anyone into believing you have a waist when you thought you didn't, your hips are slim and trim when you know they are not, and you can look 20 pounds lighter overnight!

We're Talking Deception!

Many large women remain innocents in the game of disguise mainly because, until this book, they haven't had advice targeted at them. Instead, they subject themselves to a succession of stop-and-go diets, and take up and abandon every new exercise regime which promises to shrink inches off their hips and thighs. They remain ignorant of the easiest ways in which to look healthier and more beautiful, as well as slimmer. By learning the arts of enhancement and deception that we as image consultants employ every day, you too can look wonderful without having to diet again (unless you want to lose some extra pounds), without having to exercise any more than you do normally (unless you want to feel fitter), and without spending more money (unless you get so excited with what you discover that you've just got to)!

First, you've got to be honest with yourself. How happy are you with your body and your present image? When you've answered the questionnaires in Chapter One, you will see whether your self-image is intact and your style only needs some polish, or whether it's time to come out of the shadows, look in the mirror and start to make the most of yourself. Are you a sizeist yourself? Do you refuse to try on clothes that would make you look much better than the size you normally wear simply because of the number on the label inside? Learn why sizes are totally arbitrary and ridiculous. See how the modern female shape differs significantly from its counterparts of the last 30 years.

In Chapter Two you will also discover your true Body Shape. We've updated these shapes from recent research and measurements taken of contemporary women. You may be surprised to discover that the traditional Hourglass and Pear-shape figures are slowly becoming extinct. No matter what your shape is, or what shape you are in, our tricks for making the most of your figure and proportions will save you hours of frustrating shopping. With each Body Shape we give advice on fabrics, colours, tailoring and details that will enhance your shape and balance your proportions.

Styles have changed so much over the past few years, and so too have the amount of colours and styles available to larger women. But short women who are also large still have difficulty in finding clothes to fit properly. In Chapter Three, the 'little but large' get tips on adapting and altering standard sizes to suit them.

Specific figure challenges are covered in Chapter Four, with an illustrated glossary of possibilities. Follow our advice and no-one need ever know that you have a small bust, a wide neck or bulky calves.

Chapter Five will take you through the basic 'underpinnings' that can make or break your look. Women are all different, but you will learn how to measure yourself as well as how to ask for free advice from experts. They can help you select the best undergarments to make your clothes look super.

We could not write a book without giving you advice on colour. In Chapter Six you will learn how to use colour to your advantage. First of all, if you have not already been to Color Me Beautiful, you'll learn which palette of colours suits you best. The right colours make you look healthier and draw attention to where you want it; how you *wear* those colours can make you look inches taller and inches thinner. Experiment with your own wardrobe and find out how a few new colourful additions can transform your look overnight.

Accessories, make-up, hair and grooming are all discussed, finishing touches which are vital for your overall look. Often something as simple as learning how to apply your blusher better, or how to style your hair more effectively, can make a huge difference and give you greater confidence in your appearance.

Your size should never inhibit you from enjoying life to the full. Hence, if you haven't built exercise into your life, I hope you will after reading the fun options for toning-up and feeling terrific in Chapter Nine.

If you want more confidence in yourself, if you are tired of looking the same day in, day out, if you think it's high time the world took more notice of you and all you have to offer, then don't put this book down until you've made a list of ten new steps you plan to take to make your new image a reality. Together we can make it happen.

CHAPTER 1

INNER YOU, OUTER IMAGE

All bigger women have a catalogue of stories, heart-breaking as well as laughable, which are associated with their size. Some of the most hurtful experiences were recounted for the first anniversary issue of Britain's *YES!*, the spirited magazine devoted to bigger women.

Mary Evans Young said, 'When I was fifteen, I went out with a boy who became amorous. He told me I was lovely, that I had a beautiful face . . . and that if I lost weight I would be really gorgeous!'

Editor Janice Bhend remembered, 'What springs to mind is how easily simple, everyday pleasures can be spoiled. I'll never forget having a lovely new pink bicycle. I was about nine or ten. I was so proud of it and cycled happily off down the road, when a group of boys shouted, "Ever seen an elephant on a bicycle?" It ruined my day, and my self-confidence.'

But such hurtful encounters can and are being redressed by a new spirit of self-esteem and assuredness in more and more women who are proud of themselves and their stature.

Angela Sandler of *YES!* says that, 'Fairly recently, I was at a party. I reached for something calorific and a woman said, "shouldn't you be watching your weight?" I didn't flinch, but asked if she shouldn't be watching her manners!'

Full-figured fitness expert, Astrid Longhurst, recalls meeting a friend who asked what she was up to. She reported that she had recently done some modelling. To which the friend nastily replied, 'Do a good line in rent-a-tents, do they?' Astrid's winning response was to tell her friend to check out the next day's *Daily Telegraph*.

THE BIG STEP

Bigger women all over the world are today taking steps to make the most of what they have got. Despite being a little *under*confident about their bodies, many are plunging into the beauty salons, boutiques, hairdressers, health clubs and image studios, and are experimenting with developing their outer image to build their self-esteem. Some are so motivated by their own personal development that they become aspirational models and image consultants themselves.

Many top Color Me Beautiful personnel have surprised me with stories of their fear in even approaching us to train as image consultants. Ann, formerly a successful florist, recounts being so enthusiastic after having her own colours analysed, that she was keen to start another business involving colour. Instead of working with flowers, though, she wanted to work with people. 'I filled out the application form, but couldn't bring myself to send it. My husband was the one who insisted that I did. You see, I hate rejection. But I couldn't imagine Color Me Beautiful wanting a large-size image consultant.'

Ann, a top CMB Image Consultant, at work in her studio

Ann was surprised by the reception she received at CMB where she was told that we needed more terrific women like herself to convince others that they too could look super. She was also reticent about succeeding as an image consultant, despite being accepted for

training. Would clients take advice from a larger woman? Although naturally shy and self-denying, Ann blossomed in no time into a compelling public speaker and award-winning consultant with an image that is inspirational to women of every size and shape.

Being bigger, fatter and larger than other women shapes a woman's life and her sense of self-worth. For too long women have been subjected to the tyranny of thinness as if thin meant everything. Erica Jong, the voluptuous author with no fear of being large, argues that it's women who perpetuate the notion that thin is sexy, and that size is associated with class – 'the lower the class, the fatter the arse', or that you could never be too rich or too thin. Men, as Erica knows well, love flesh!

That Competitive Spirit

Women have been competing with each other for centuries, and the main competitive arena has been beauty and fashion. Even though many women today are channelling that competitive spirit into the workplace, most of us still work hard at holding our own in the everyday beauty contest with colleagues, friends, sisters and strangers.

Many women see others in relation to themselves. Our body obsessions become a daily measuring game to see how much firmer, longer, slimmer, fuller, higher and lower other women's bits are when compared to our own! We'd all be liars if we didn't admit to sizing other women up from time to time. I've got an obsession with legs, having been short-changed genetically with rather stubby numbers. For the flat-chested, the cup size of other comparable women is their focus. For the tall, it's the petite. For the wobbly, it's the firm. For the redheads it's the blondes. The competitive game goes on and on.

Women who become obsessive, assessing their bodies constantly against others, generally harbour a notion about what is the *ideal* body, or beauty. Any of you who has lived through a phase of low self-esteem, when this sort of preoccupation can be rampant, will know that focussing on anything that is ideal, which is probably unattainable therefore, only leaves you feeling hopelessly inadequate.

Your Body Image

Psychiatrists today agree that there has been a dramatic increase in eating disorders in the last 30 years, mainly because of the growing number of us who are dissatisfied with our bodies.

The term *body image* refers to the internal subjective feeling we have about our bodies and, consequently, how we think we appear to others. Our body image contributes to the direction our lives take, as how we feel about our bodies determines the image we have of ourselves and, hence, our self-esteem. Our amount of self-esteem determines the confidence with which we tackle the opportunities and challenges that life throws at us.

However, understanding what we really feel about our bodies is not straightforward. Our body image fluctuates over time – like a yo-yo through puberty, for instance – and can be positive when in a good relationship, less so when in a bad one or when feeling alone. We all think less of our bodies before and during our periods. If you add up all those weeks of feeling lousy over a lifetime, that's an extra thirteen or fourteen years of poor body image, thanks to Mother Nature and her hormones!

Let's face it, we are totally irrational about our body image. When some of us get preoccupied with being *fat* we may be totally wrong. Our weight may have very little to do with our measure of actual body fat – about half of female body weight is water anyway. So if we feel *fat*, then diet and lose weight quickly, it is probably due to dehydration (losing some of the water), not by making any real inroads on the fat.

And what are we striving for anyway? To look like a stick insect? Only 5 per cent of women are as thin as the models in the glossy magazines, and you can imagine how much fun they'd be to spend an evening with! Most of us can recount tales of meeting such *creatures* – for that's what they are, not real women, but specimens unto themselves. Yet too many women suffer from unrealistic goals for their own bodies, and the media perpetuates them. Every fashion season they throw armies of anorexic young things at us, as if theirs were the images we should all try to attain.

Why not try to evaluate your own body image today? Answer the following questions according to how you feel right now, and not how you know you know you feel when you are on top of the world or down in the dumps. Give it a go, and discover if you have a healthy self-image or one needing work to prove to yourself and others that you are wonderful.

Body Image Scale

Each statement is followed by two possible responses: first Agree, and second Disagree. Tick or circle the one that best describes how you feel, A or B, depending on whether you agree or disagree. Respond to every statement. If not completely sure which response is more accurate, select the more appropriate.

Don't cheat by reading the scoring explanation before completing the questionnaire. Do not spend too much time on each statement. Try to be as honest as possible.

	Agree / Disagree	
1. Most of my energy goes to controlling my weight	A	B
2. If I could change my life, I would not start with my body	B	A
3. I do envy how other women can look so good	A	B
4. My weight will stay fine in the future	B	A
5. Any weight gain for me is unacceptable	A	B

	Agree/Disagree	
6. I don't mind trying on bathing suits in a shop	B	A
7. Staying hungry is good discipline	A	B
8. I enjoy intimacy	B	A
9. Anything that upsets my dieting upsets me	A	B
10. I don't mind lying on a beach full of attractive people in swimming costumes	B	A

Work out your score by adding up the numbers of As and Bs you have ticked or circled.

If the number of As equal 7 or more Your body image isn't what you deserve. Be honest: are you preoccupied with thinness, weight and food? Bets are that you have a fixed idea of what your weight should be, and you believe that if you achieve it you will be happy. Maybe you have been that 'wonder weight' once before. Were you really happy? Wasn't your life consumed by the demon diet, counting calories and restricting your happiness? Naturally you chucked it all in.

Your goal now should not be a certain weight or dress size, unless you are so overweight your health is in jeopardy. You are going to learn such wonderful things about looking and feeling terrific in this book that you'll be happy to toss those scales away for good.

If the number of As is between 5 and 7 Okay, you aren't depressed about your body, but you still give yourself too much of a hard time. You have been through the dieting dilemma as well, and you may have upset your metabolic rate so much that it's even harder to lose weight today than it was a few years ago. So let's forget about calories and think healthy eating, living and being beautiful. You deserve nothing less.

If the number of As is between 3 and 5 Your body image is on a par with most women, but is influenced by your self-confidence. If you are having a tough time at work or perhaps a special relationship has soured, you've blamed yourself. Come on, girl. Nothing is that simple or that complicated. When life takes a downturn you've got to analyse what went wrong, *separately* from who you are and what you look like. Look at all the 'beautiful people' who are absolutely miserable. Now doesn't that cheer you up?!

If the number of As is between 0 and 2 A big gold star is in order:

you've got a great body image. Chances are you love to cook, and enjoy a meal with friends far more than fitting into a lycra mini-skirt. You are free from dieting and confident in who you are. You know that fulfilment has more to do with loving, learning and doing, than with counting calories or having a waist the size of a nine year old. Try and spread some of your enthusiasm for life and your positive attitude to other women with a poorer body image.

Image Matters

The body is only one part of your image, the overall impression you make on others. Now we need to explore your personal appearance in a wider context to incorporate all aspects of your look from your grooming, hair and make-up, to your clothes. Being bigger presents a wealth of possibilities as well as challenges when it comes to dressing. Finding the right size, at the right price, in a good colour, of a nice fabric and quality construction, isn't easy. It's even more difficult if you are busy and don't have ready access to outlets that suit your scale as well as your budget.

Your image involves a composite picture. It involves the tangible bits like your earrings, the cut of your clothes and the colour of your lipstick. It also involves the *in*tangible aspects, like how you walk into a room, and the confidence in your voice. In this book, we are going to focus on the tangible things that you can do to make the most of yourself. The chances are, that if you begin to feel terrific about how you look, then the intangibles will follow: you will carry yourself better, you'll be more confident about meeting new people, and you will speak up for yourself, knowing that you are worth everyone's attention.

Let's see how together you are with your own image. Answer the following questions, ticking a Yes or a No, and see if you are doing yourself justice.

How Together Is Your Image?

	Yes	No
1. Can you list your three best features?	☐	☐
2. Do you enjoy wearing both skirts and trousers?	☐	☐
3. If you could afford it, would you select some lovely fabric and have an outfit made to your own specifications?	☐	☐

4. When shopping for clothes, do you go to the department or section appropriate for your size? ☐ ☐

5. Do you take care of your skin with a good skin-care routine or even the occasional facial? ☐ ☐

6. Do you only go to the hairdresser when your hair has grown out of control? ☐ ☐

7. Do you know which style of swimming costume is most flattering on you? ☐ ☐

8. When you purchase clothes that don't exactly fit – perhaps needing to get a larger size to be more comfortable only to find the length and sleeves too long – do you spend a bit extra in having them altered to look perfect? ☐ ☐

9. When you get dressed in the morning, do you review your image in a full-length mirror? ☐ ☐

10. Do you use colour mainly as camouflage? ☐ ☐

11. Are accessories the key to your look? ☐ ☐

12. Do you spend more than 10 minutes getting ready in the morning (not including a bath/shower)? ☐ ☐

13. As you can't always find the latest looks in your size, do you dismiss fashion trends altogether as irrelevant for you? ☐ ☐

14. Do you avoid occasions for formal dress as you don't have anything that would look appropriate? ☐ ☐

15. If friends invited you to join them on a gentle walking holiday in Tuscany, would you decline because you felt you couldn't keep up the pace? ☐ ☐

16. Are you guilty about the amount of money you spend on your image? ☐ ☐

Answers to Questionnaire

1. **Yes** Of course you know your best features. Why stop at three?

2. **Yes** Your size should not preclude you from wearing skirts or trousers. Availability of what you want is the only obstacle, but thankfully that is now changing for the better.

3. **Yes** To treat yourself to something special, something that you know would be flattering and give you lots of pleasure as well as use, might be the smartest choice instead of exhausting yourself in futile pursuit, only to settle for something less than wonderful. After reading this book and learning your best colours and styles, you can direct a good dressmaker or tailor to make your dream look come true.

4. **Yes and No** No would be wrong if you hover in clothes departments in the hope of squeezing into things that won't be flattering. But if you answered **No** because you like to see how the latest fashions are put together, to help you with selecting the most current looks from your own department, then you get a point.

5. **Yes** Taking care of your skin means you want attention on your face – the centre of communication. There are details of how to achieve a glowing skin in Chapter Eight.

6. **No** You should pay careful attention to your hair. Your hair frames your face, and is potentially one of your greatest assets. There are more tips on selecting the best style in Chapter Eight.

7. **Yes** Your size should not prevent you from enjoying swimming or a holiday in the sun. The best style is not simply one that fits – you've got to learn what possibilities are most flattering on you. See Chapter Five for details.

8. **Yes** You are killing your image and wasting money if you don't spend that bit extra on making the outfit perfect for *you*. See details on achieving your best fit in Chapter 4.

9. **Yes** You should be able to admire and criticise the effect of your image from head to toe.

10. **No** You should wear colours that flatter you, not make you disappear.

11. **Yes** Accessories, like colour, draw attention to where you want it. If you aren't exploiting your best features, then you are letting your image down.

12. **Yes**   To present your best every day takes more than 10 minutes. At best, you should spend 20 minutes and never feel indulgent if you take 30, only proud that you are doing yourself justice.

13. **No**   Sure it's a bore when you want a certain look, but can't find it. You will learn in this book how you can achieve any current look by analysing the key features and putting it together yourself.

14. **No**   If your life offers promise of some fancy parties, then you need to get some options ready. The key will be learning how to choose the most flattering options for your shape and personality. Read on.

15. **No**   Why should your size and fitness prevent you from enjoying yourself and your friends? Don't use your size as the reason to miss out on adventures. If you aren't fit enough to participate in moderate exercise, it's time to take yourself in hand. See Chapter Nine.

16. **No**   Every woman should invest in herself, realising that her image affects her self-esteem and the reactions she gets from others. Looking good doesn't require a lot of money, only knowing how to get the best out of your investments.

Now, after coming to grips with your body image, and finding out how together your overall image is, it's time to get down to learning how you can make even more of yourself. You are going to learn how to wear clothes that make the most of your figure, shape and proportions. And we begin with your notion of size which you will discover is all relative . . . But you need convincing, so read on.

CHAPTER 2

SHAPE, NOT SIZE, MATTERS

Open your wardrobe and inspect the labels inside your skirts. Are they all the same? Probably not. There are two, the same size, bought from your favourite shop two years ago. But the skirts from the same shop this year seem a lot more generous. You haven't lost weight and wish you had bought a smaller size. Then there's the expensive American number which boasts a label three sizes smaller than your usual UK size. Sure, you know that American sizes are different. The labels tell us that they should be just one size off from the British, not three! Two skirts, purchased from different mail-order catalogues are the same size, but one you can hardly zip up while the other is a sure bet to get you through the worst days of the month. Are you some freak of nature?

How often I have heard women apologise for their 'malformed bodies' that don't fit into standard sizes and shapes. 'My hips are impossible. When I find a skirt to cover them I am stuck with excess inches at the waist.' Or, 'I always need to buy a larger jacket to accommodate my full bust. Of course, doing so means always having to chop inches off the sleeves and the shoulders are usually massive. But I have to live with the best I can get.'

Research both in the UK and Germany confirms that most women, whatever their size, have trouble with fit. Here are the main problems:

- Unable to fasten zips at the waist
- Waistbands dip on skirts and trousers
- Blouses gape at the bust
- Darts seem to be in the wrong position
- Skirts ride up because they are too tight
- Necklines are too wide
- Sleeve lengths are too long and shoulders out of place

No Such Thing as a Standard Size

Take heart. There is nothing wrong with you, it's the system that's crazy. Indeed there are no standardised sizes in Britain, America or most countries. In Britain, the last time there was an attempt to set a standard was in the 1950s. Remember the films and documentaries from that era? Think of how slight the women *and the men* were. Remember the times. It was post-war and there was food-rationing. There were no such things as convenience foods or junk foods, hence people consumed far fewer calories daily than we do today. In the 1950s, women were also more active, not with leisure pursuits, but in running the home, shopping, taking care of children, etc. Few had cars to pop down to the shops, and most walked everywhere. So, the combined effect of diet and lifestyle meant that they were a quite different size and shape from the women of the 1990s.

But the measurements from the 1950s have been the basis of sizing for the last 40 years. Or have they? In reality, designers and manufacturers have taken things into their own hands rather than wait for governments to conduct the proper surveys. Over the years, most have made 'concessions' to the basic sizings, adding ease and inches here and there without letting the customers in on the secret. When styles or 'the looks' change, tailoring becomes more or less restrictive, which causes havoc when you are trying to get a good fit.

My, How We've Changed!

36-24-36. The fantasy hourglass figure, with the waist at least 10 in (25 cm) smaller than the bust and hips. This was the original UK size 12 pattern set in the 1950s when the first and only national measurement survey was conducted in Britain. The only measurements recorded were three – the bust, the waist and the hips – which became the basis of today's sizing system.

Last year one mail-order company, J.D. Williams, fed up with the high returns on its catalogue business due to 'wrong fit', decided to re-measure today's female. Over 700 women of all ages (19–90), sizes (12–30), backgrounds and locations were measured in more than 70 places on their bodies to produce new patterns. A total of 50,765 measurements were fed into a computer to produce the new sizings.

Initially, they couldn't believe the numbers. 'These will never fit a size 14!' said veteran pattern cutter, Vic Ettenfield, 'the cut is completely different.' After extensive testing, they proved that Vic was wrong and the computer was right.

Blue – Typical mid 30s female form in 1950s
Pink – Typical mid 30s female form in 1990s

Compared to the existing standard sizes, today's women have:

- larger, lower breasts
- a thicker waist
- larger upper hips
- a more rounded tummy
- fuller upper arms
- larger rib cage
- a flatter bottom

This survey confirmed similar findings to one conducted in Germany showing that only 10 per cent of the population were comfortable in the standard sizes!

YOUNG SIZES

Another catch in getting the right size is the difference between clothes designed for young women and those for older women. Larger young girls despair at not being able to fit into trendy designs which are always inches more skimpy in every size. Their only bet for a decent pair of jeans is to resort to wearing the same label as their mum. Not a groovy alternative for a teenager!

Generally 'young' clothes also equate with less expensive clothes. When clothes are cheaper the manufacturer has made savings everywhere, especially in the fabric and tailoring.

ABOVE LEFT Trendy styles worn by smaller teens are available now in every size. However bigger girls should take care in selecting the most flattering as well as the most current look.

ABOVE RIGHT All teenagers adopt the uniform of their peers. Natasha has the accepted look, but is it flattering on her?

Young, current and comfy. Perfect!

As a rule, good-quality labels afford more generous sizing. The posher the American label, for example, the smaller the size you can get, yes, up to three smaller than the British. However, the *style* will still be ample, because American designers build extra inches into the hips to accommodate the fuller American backside. American clothes are huge, but make you feel terrific as the sizes are all 'small'!

Leading international retailer Marks & Spencer commissioned its own study of women's bodies and came up with a new mannequin, developed using a three-dimensional body-shape scan of 155 women. The mannequin's name is 'Annie Murphy', who presently represents Ms Average, and guides all their designers and patternmakers to improve the fit of new-style clothing and lingerie.

I can always get an accurate idea of a woman's size, when needing to dress her for a photoshoot in the UK, if I ask her in what size Marks & Spencer skirt or dress she is most comfortable. With this benchmark, I can select clothes from M & S or any other make going up and down the sizes, knowing how the clothes will fit her. Every country has its benchmark labels which are reliable guides to a woman's real size.

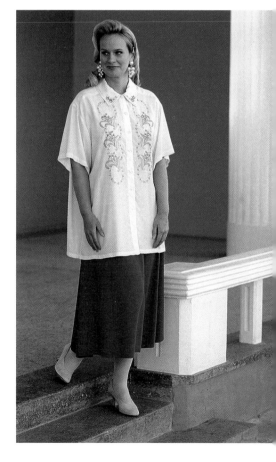

BELOW Larger women aren't shapeless so it's wrong to assume they should wear shapeless clothes. When you know your body shape you can select styles that complement your figure best.

Think Shape, Not Size

If sizing is so relative then there's little point in caring about what size clothes you wear, so long as the fit is right and the style is flattering. To save you time and effort trying on unsuitable styles, you need first to discover your basic body shape.

The accompanying chart shows the six basic body shapes for women over a size 16 (12/14 USA/Canada). To determine which shape describes yours most closely follow these guidelines:

• Assess your shape in a leotard, body or bathing suit. Not because it's too depressing to do it in only a bra and panties, but because you can't often distinguish the silhouette (outline of your body shape) as easily as you can in a one-piece costume.

• Use a full-length mirror to get an accurate overall impression. For best results try a good three-way mirror in a department store.

• Get a second opinion from an honest friend. Our own ability to be objective can be limited.

Consider Your Scale

In addition to basic body shape, image consultants also take another factor into consideration when selecting the best size for a woman. This is her *scale* – her height and bone structure. If a woman has a large frame, i.e. big bones, she always looks better in a looser fit or even a size larger to compliment herself. We call her look *overscale*. Neat-fitting clothes are better on women with smaller bones.

Height is a factor in selecting your size, not simply for getting a good fit, but for the clothes to balance with your build. The taller you are the more flattered you will be in generously cut clothes. So, as with your bone structure your height can also make you *overscale* – i.e. a woman who looks better in larger patterns, more texture and an easy fit. Shorter women can look swamped in loose-fitting styles and, regardless of their shape, are better in more honed designs. More specific advice for enhancing the scale of the 'little but large' woman is covered in Chapter Three.

Here are some guidelines for determining if you are overscale, not necessarily overweight. First take your wrist measurement, then check your height in the chart below. If your wrist measures 6¹/₂ in (16 cm) or more, and your weight falls into the range given in the chart for your height, you are overscale.

Wrist measurement 6¹/₂ in (16 cm) and over

Height	Weight Range
5ft 7in (1.7m)	140lb (63kg) – 154lbs (70kg)
5ft 8in (1.73m)	142lbs (65kg) – 160lbs (73kg)
5ft 9in (1.75m)	145lbs (65kg) – 164lbs (75kg)
5ft 10in (1.78m)	148lbs (67kg) – 168lbs (76kg)
5ft 11in (1.8m)	150lbs (68kg) – 173lbs (79kg)
6ft (1.83m)	155lbs (70kg) – 177lbs (80kg)
6ft 1in (1.85m)	158lbs (71kg) – 183lbs (83kg)
6ft 2in (1.88m)	160lbs (72kg) – 187lbs (85kg)

If you fit into this range, you are *overscale*, which means that you will have more freedom in working with your body shape than women who wear the same size but are shorter and fuller (though have a similar shape to you). Read the descriptions and advice for each shape and note adaptations you can make, due to being both taller and having a larger frame.

THE INVERTED TRIANGLE

Famous Examples   Bette Midler, Jennifer Saunders

You have broad straight shoulders and a full bustline, two assets most women would love to have. But you know that being so broad on the upper quarter of your body makes finding clothes very difficult. This, teamed with having a narrower waist and neat hips, means you often buy clothes on the top two sizes bigger than you need on the bottom. You are the queen of the separates department!

Don't Disguise

Your figure is wonderful when we are able to appreciate your striking silhouette. Make the most of your neat bottom half in well-tailored trousers and skirts, never hide yourself under masses of fabric. When you keep the top long and simple and the bottom neat, you look your most interesting.

As you have natural, built-in 'shoulder pads', avoid any tops or jackets that add bulk or width there. Raglan, rather than set-in, sleeves will minimise the strength of your shoulders which, if exaggerated, can look masculine. Fabrics in your tops should be fluid, and drape over your bust and torso. If the fabrics are too stiff, your shoulders and bust will be emphasised.

Watch the Waist

Often women with your figure have shorter torsos or little waist area. Hence, even if your figure is trim, you want to avoid waisted styles as they will only make you look fuller on the top. A simple overblouse will be more flattering than one tucked in. As you know, a full bust is always exaggerated as soon as you wear anything too belted.

Jackets

Single-breasted jackets will be more slimming than double-breasted styles as their peaked lapels, in effect, broaden your shoulders and add more to your bustline. Avoid classic blazers in preference to easier, less constructed shapes. Always look for some tapering at the waist, but – more important – at the hip line. If the jacket is too boxy, no-one will fully appreciate your figure.

As your legs are probably long in proportion to your body, and also

Inverted Triangle

because of your full bust, longer length jackets will be more flattering on you than shorter styles.

Skirts

Even if you are a large size, avoid full, gathered skirts. These are the ones that disguise your stunning silhouette. Your flat bottom and hips will be great in straight or wrap skirts. Sure, some easing in the waist band is fine. Just avoid too much bulk there. Simple knit or lycra blends in a straight design or knife pleats are some of your best choices.

Your proportions mean that you can also consider skirts with hemline detail, i.e. like kick pleats or tiered. You could even sport a 'fish tail' hemline, perhaps for evening.

Trousers

If your lifestyle and personality allow, trousers will be flattering for you whether for work, play or evening. From lean leggings to palazzo pants you will be terrific in most styles. Team them with simple big shirts, long jumpers or waistcoats or try a sheer, lace or satin top in your favourite colour for evening.

Dresses

Buying dresses from department stores has been frustrating for you. To be comfortable on the top, you end up with masses of extra fabric on the bottom. If you find a terrific style that is a simple straight cut, consider getting it if you can have it tapered, from the hips to the hem.

Otherwise your best bet for wearing dresses successfully is to select the patterns of your choice and find a good dressmaker or tailor who can adapt it to your shape.

LEFT A flattering casual look for the Inverted Triangle shape.

Colours and Patterns

You can wear colours of your choice on the top and bottom. Where other body shapes are advised to keep all the detail on the top, you want to be careful and not go for too much detail in the bust or shoulder area. So, no appliqué or beading, for example, in your blouses. If you like texture, e.g. lace, keep it soft and fluid. Avoid stiff, starchy fabrics in your blouses.

Accessory Tips

Necklaces   Keep them long and simple. If you wear a large pendant, so fashionable recently, you may look as though you have a third breast! A few chains worn together or several strands of beads can be interesting without being too obvious.

Brooches   You don't need added details here, so avoid them.

Scarves   Long oblong scarves or large shawls are your best bets. Wear them draped around the neck, hanging in two vertical splashes of colour.

Belts   If you have a neat waist and hips, try wearing belts slung lower than your waist for best effect. Chain belts or sash styles are particularly flattering on your shape.

Shoes   As you probably have longer legs in proportion to your body, you can have fun with shoes. Boots of any length are also attractive on your shape.

Handbags   Large-style shoulder bags you can easily accommodate, while anything too small might look a bit ridiculous against your striking stature.

THE STRAIGHT BODY SHAPE

Famous Examples   Allison Moyet, Barbara Bush, Claire Rayner, Vanessa Feltz

You have the most popular shape of all. Most women over size 16 (12/14 USA and Canada) have shoulders and hips which are about the same dimension and their waists are not well defined. Often this is due to having a broad rib cage and, possibly, a short waist. You are also the type who puts weight on in the middle, as opposed to the thighs. So, you are usually blessed with great legs.

Straight Body Shape

The Straight Body shape can apply to women who are somewhat 'overweight' as well as to women who have larger frames and are taller. You will be the *overscaled* Straight Body if you have one of the profiles (height/weight/wrist measurements) listed on page 26.

Yours is an easy shape to dress provided you accept your own features and work with them rather than try to be a shape that you are not. Women with Straight Body shapes always swear that in their next life they are going to come back with a waist!

Simplicity Is the Key

Yours is an elegant shape when dressed according to your lines. Even if you love frills and flounces you must resist the urge to wear them in main items, and only have them in details like the cuffs on your sleeves or a hankie in a breast pocket, especially if you are average to shorter in stature. Your body shape is more flattered by elegant yet uncomplicated designs and easy lines. This does not mean that you can't have fun with beautiful patterns and textures. Of course you can, provided that the designs are simple.

If you are an *overscale* Straight Body type, you will be able to handle more detail but still you will find uncluttered designs more flattering.

Jackets

The worst disasters in your wardrobe are the fitted jackets, short or long, and anything with fussy details like a peplum. Belted designs are possible provided that they are a soft sash as opposed to a stiff buckled number. A belted design is best if it ties slightly below your natural waistline.

Your best jackets can be either single or double-breasted, long and lean. Non-vented or side-vented styles are both possible on you. The amount of padding at the shoulders you can tolerate will depend on your overall size. If you are short to average in height, a little padding might be good to make the hips appear slimmer. If you are tall, beware of any excess of padding as they might make you look a bit severe.

Your straight silhouette welcomes layering, provided you don't use heavy or bulky pieces. Try a body suit, then a shirt and add a waistcoat to wear over your skirts and trousers. One of your most flattering options will be to wear a long, cardigan style jacket (to the knee or longer) over skirts or trousers.

OPPOSITE Long-line single-breasted jackets are the straight body shape's best bet. If your legs are an asset, show them off in simple, straight skirts.

Skirts

Full, gathered or tiered styles break down your striking silhouette and just make you look chunky. Who needs that? Elasticated waists will be fine provided that the cut is straight. A few inverted pleats either side of the tummy for comfort will be much more flattering than a waistband with gathers all the way round.

Try pleated styles – drop-waisted or knife pleats as opposed to box pleats which will be too 'heavy' in appearance, and make you look fuller than you are over the hips and thighs.

If you are tall and/or long in the legs, long-length skirts will be optional, in addition to shorter skirts which you can hem to the most flattering part of the leg. Simply ask yourself if your knees are worth a view or not, then decide on the best length. (Where the leg naturally indents below the knee is often a good spot.)

If your tummy girth is full, avoid stiff fabrics like gabardine, linen or denim in skirts in preference to styles that will drape more easily over your abdomen. Even though you know you will be best in longer tops, and don't like to have your tummy on full view, it's still better to be comfortable.

Dresses

The chemise style or coat dress will be your best option, and make the most of your straight lines. If you hanker after something with more interest, resist the urge. Try one of these in a wow colour then work on adding some striking accessories to make it memorable.

The drop-waist style dress is another alternative provided that you don't have short legs.

Trousers

Classic, tailored cuts will flatter you most, along with simple fluid designs that have an elasticated waistline and fall straight. Jean-style trousers make the most of your great legs and you the envy of many other large women. For comfort, choose jeans and casual trousers that have some lycra in the fabric mixture.

Colours and Patterns

Your height will dictate how wild you can go in patterns on the bottom half. If in doubt, keep the patterns on the bottom negligible, i.e. subtle self-weave mixtures that look like a plain colour from a distance but up close reveal a pattern.

If you are a plump Straight Body shape, you are best with a modest amount of texture on the top in your blouses and jackets. So, a double knit with a bit of detail will be preferable to a big mohair sweater that will only make you look fuller. Taller women with larger frames can carry off more texture and larger designs, but are advised not to wear too many layers when they do. A chunky jumper with a bold pattern is better on its own than under a jacket or over a thick polo.

Accessory Tips

Necklaces   They will be great on you but most effective if you keep them simple and striking. The longer the chain the better.

Brooches   Keep them geometric rather than round and too traditional. You want to play up your angular lines and do so best with striking pieces. Keep the size of these and other ornamental accessories in relation to your size. The taller you are the more you can pile them on.

Scarves   If your neck is long and bosom not too ample, use scarves to create interest with your simple tops and elegant jackets.

Belts   Avoid altogether if you carry weight at the waist. If trim, keep the colour the same as your skirt or wear one low on the hips over your blouses.

Shoes   Your elegant style requires up-to-date shoes. Don't cheat here. Flats or heels (except the very high) are both for you.

Handbags   Big, sloppy bags will jar against your striking, straight physique. Keep it sharp with an envelope-style purse or well-structured 'shopping' shoulder bag.

THE HOURGLASS SHAPE

Famous Examples   Oprah Winfrey, Natalie Cole, Sophia Loren, 'Bet Lynch' (Julie Goodyear)

Even when you may be carrying some extra weight you still have a defined feminine shape of a full bust, accentuated waist and full hips. Your bust and hips are about the same measurement and your waist is at least 8 in (20 cm) smaller. To look your best, and slimmest, requires that you play up these features, not disguise them. This does not mean that you must wear tight or constricting styles that are agony to wear for more than a few hours. No, just appreciate that the cut of your clothes should follow the contours of your body.

Show That Waist

Your waist is an important feature of your shape and one that you should accentuate to look your best. Even though you are a large size, you want all your clothes to taper at the waist. If they don't you will look as if you are hiding a big tummy and look fatter than you are.

Jackets

Think tailored femininity when you select your jackets. If your bust is full, keep the styling over the chest minimal and avoid very cinched styles in favour of gently waisted designs. If your bust is average, and you are a smaller size (16–18; 14-16 USA and Canada) then you can choose more fitted styles that have darts in all the right places to define your feminine contours.

If you are a taller Hourglass, beware of very figure-hugging designs. Try the next size up in your jackets. Remember an easier fit will be more feminine and slimming. Should your proportions allow, i.e. you aren't short in the waist, consider a peplum on your jacket, perhaps for a more formal occasion.

The fabrics for your jackets can be textured like tweed, jacquard velvet or suede, provided that they aren't too stiff. Wool crepe, knits and heavy silks, like stonewashed, will drape more effectively over your curvy figure without adding width to your silhouette.

The length of your jacket will depend on your bottom. If it protrudes, make the jacket cover the hips. If it is neater you can opt for either short or longer jackets.

Hourglass Shape

33

Skirts

Your feminine shape can take either straight or softly gathered skirts. Sarong or softly-wrapped styles are particularly good. The important aspect to watch for is ease of movement over the hips and tummy area. If the waist isn't elasticated, look for soft gathers only in the front or back. Side pleats on either side of the tummy will also give you the comfort you require.

Always try on a straight skirt before buying it. Sit down in it for a minute or two. If it rides up while you are seated then the cut is too skimpy for your shape (better on a Straight Body type). Or if you get those horizontal 'stretch marks' across the thighs when seated, which will become etched in as wrinkles as soon as you stand up, then the cut and/or fabric are not for you. Some straight skirts with elastication at the back or sides can work, but the fabric should still be able to drape over your curves.

Long full, tiered or pleated skirts are attractive on you in preference to definite A-line skirts which will take attention away from your most flattering regions above.

Trousers

To make the most of your figure, you should avoid straight, classic-cut trousers in tightly woven materials as they will only make you look chunky not curvy. Soft wools, cotton/wool or silk jersey, knits and washed silk will drape your figure best. Even if the trousers don't have belt loops, finish off your trousers with a nice belt to show off your waist. If you like comfy overblouses with your trousers, also use a belt for best effect.

ABOVE Stylish and shapely! This is possible for all hourglass body shapes, provided the fabric is soft and the cut fitted.

Dresses

The Hourglass body shape is perfect for dresses if they suit your personality and lifestyle. For work, they make a welcome change from separates, and are so comfortable. Always remember to team them with a jacket for the office to project a professional image.

Coat dresses will be fine if in softer fabrics, so long as they have some waist definition (like a sash or back belt at the waist). Better yet will be shirtwaisted styles or soft, wrap dresses that always require a belt.

Colours and Patterns

If you like patterns, use them in one of two ways. First for effect in one piece, like the blouse under a jacket, a pretty scarf set against a plain background, or in the jacket when keeping the blouse and skirt plain. This will focus the eye on what you might consider your most flattering area, and if on the top, the pattern will also draw attention to your face.

Patterns and proportions – get them right for you. Checks can look strained over curves and have an unsuccessful effect.

Another way you can incorporate patterns from head to toe is with a two-piece dress, or a long waistcoat and matching trousers. The key to wearing patterns head-to-toe is for them not to be too large or too obvious (i.e. a striking colour combination). If you do the latter, the attention is on the wild pattern and *you* will be lost. Subtle patterns in your best colours that are average in scale (not too small) will be the best.

The same is true of wearing your brightest colours. Focus them as 'attention-getters' where you want them. As with patterns, avoid wearing the brightest and lightest colours in your trousers and skirts. You will look really elegant in monochromatic blends of colours, i.e. toning various shades of the same colour throughout. For example, try navy trousers with a blue-grey jacket and blouse set off with a wonderful scarf in a rainbow of blue and grey tones.

RIGHT Of course you can wear patterned skirts. Here is how to put one together with separates for a great result.

Accessory Tips

Necklaces   Choker to medium-length necklaces will be flattering. Longer length chains can be worn if you aren't too full-busted.

Brooches   Will be attractive when you wear the most simple dress or jacket. Only team one with a necklace *and* earrings if you are average to tall in height. If in doubt, wear the brooch only with a pair of earrings.

Scarves   The softest wools and crepes only. Learn how to wear them cleverly over a simple blouse. But don't get too contrived with bows and big knots which will only detract from your figure.

Belts   They are the key to your look. Try softer leathers and fabric belts that you can tie yourself as opposed to very cumbersome heavy metal buckles. Chain belts are also possible. Just get one appropriate to your size. If it is too delicate it may look wrong against your figure.

Shoes   As your look will feature your feminine contours, thick, clumpy shoes will detract from it. Select more delicate styles but remember not to go too delicate for your stature, or opt for very thin or very high heels.

Handbags   Avoid stiff, boxy styles. For work, try a 'shopper' style bag for your work papers instead of a square attaché. For evening, the drawstring bag was made for you.

THE PEAR SHAPE

Famous Examples   Whoopi Goldberg, Erica Jong, Su Pollard, Penelope Keith

A Pear body shape recognises her description or body shape faster than any other type. She has had to live with the challenge of full hips and thighs which are often one, two or even three sizes larger than her top. Take heart. Where you carry your weight causes less strain on the heart than the gals who have thick waists but slim thighs. So, that's a major compensation.

Some women eventually develop the Pear shape with age. It is well documented that after childbirth and the menopause, many women add pounds and inches to their hips and thighs. So yours is a very natural feminine shape, even though it does have its challenges in dressing.

The Pear shape, like all others, is more challenging when you are shorter. The taller you are the easier it is to conceal the difference between the top and bottom halves; however, tall women can be terribly frustrated in finding the *lengths* they need.

First Things First

When looking for a new outfit, you are wise to start from the bottom up. Ask yourself if you want a skirt or trousers as the base, then get hunting.

BELOW So who's a pear shape then? The illusion created with contrasting colours on top and an easy-fitting darker bottom is one of your best looks.

Pear Shape

Once you get the right fabric and cut you can team it with a terrific top. It's a waste of time to fall for a stunning top only to be unable to find suitable slacks or a skirt to complete the look. By all means, get some inspiration from the jackets and tops, but hold off purchasing anything until you find the bottom bit.

Skirts

Softly gathered, slightly full skirts are needed to cover the girth over the hips. Your best option for a comfortable fit at the waistline is some or total elastication that will keep the band in place. Normal waistbands will be inches too large as you have to get bigger size skirts to cover your hips. Even when you tailor the waistband in, straight design skirts 'expose' a broad bottom more than looser designs.

Avoid A-line shirts which will make you look wider and shorter. Short/knee-length boxy skirts that fit can also be unflattering. Take one out of the wardrobe and try this tapering trick: with some straight pins, taper the side seams in slightly from mid thigh to the hem. See how slimming this is.

For best effect, don't wear your skirts or trousers on their own, i.e. with a tucked-in top. A long jacket, waistcoat, or cardigan will be flattering and help to 'build-up' your top to be more in proportion with your bottom.

Trousers

I don't need to tell you how difficult it is to get good fitting trousers. It will be trial and error and finally discovering the manufacturer for you. When you find a great pair, flattering and of good quality, get two pairs instead of one.

As with your skirts, the goal is to get the fit over the hips, tummy and bottom right first. Classically tailored styles rarely accommodate your shape. Try uncomplicated designs with a basic elasticated waist that has plenty of fabric so that the fit over the thighs is loose. You will always look slimmer in a looser rather than tight fit. Consider culottes, instead of trousers, but avoid very heavy fabrics like denim or corduroy which will only make you look heavier. Knits, jersey and viscose will drape much better.

As with your skirts, you'll want to team your trousers and culottes with a blouse, then another layer – waistcoat, shawl, long cardigan or jacket – for best effect.

Jackets

Try on a jacket from your wardrobe that you don't like. I bet I know why it doesn't work. It probably ends on the bottom or thighs where you are widest, thereby making you look even wider.

The keys to a successful jacket for a Pear shape are in the shoulders and the length. First, the length. If you are short, you have to be careful not to swamp yourself in long jackets and skirts in an attempt to cover your bottom. If you have a nice waist (an asset for many Pear shapes), then end the jacket at your hip, and select styles that are slightly fitted to identify your waist.

Average to tall Pear shapes are always better in a longer jacket. Get the length long enough to end just below the widest part of your thighs. You'll be amazed what a difference it can make. Also beware of the placement of buttons. Double-breasted models with bold buttons accentuate the width where you don't need it. So too do pockets on the jacket. Have the details above the waist to bring the eye up and out – a breast pocket, wide lapels, epaulettes, gathered shoulders, wide collars, etc.

When selecting a jacket, watch the buttons – bold, contrasting or metal buttons on double-breasted jackets catch the eye and can make you look wider.

LEFT Single-breasted styles are always more slimming.

Never leave home without **shoulder pads!** You might have been let down by Mother Nature in the shoulder department, having either very narrow shoulders or rather droopy ones. Not to worry. Just vow never to display them in full view aside from loved ones at home or on the beach.

You disguise narrow shoulders most effectively by always wearing shoulder pads. That's right, *always*. Whether they are in or out of fashion is irrelevant for you. But don't use any old shoulder pads, especially the ones in the back of the wardrobe from the mid 1980s. They are much too obvious. Your shoulder pads need to be discreet and almost indistinguishable.

Although you'll be tempted to buy your right-size jacket, even though it is a size or two smaller than your bottom, resist. Try instead the next size up. A larger jacket will be a looser fit, slightly broader than your own shoulders (you can fill that gap with your pads), but will be easier on the hips where you need it. A looser fit on top always helps to balance the scale with the bottom – you won't look so much like a Pear shape if you do! Always get the sleeves taken up to fit perfectly when necessary.

Dresses

The difference between your top and bottom half make all but two-piece styles undesirable in terms of fit and finish. As with other shapes with similar challenges, if you love dresses it might be best to line up a good dressmaker or tailor to get the fit perfect for you (taking into account some of the tips you've learned here).

Colours and Patterns

You can't be indifferent about colour, it is too important to your overall look. Use medium to dark plain colours on the bottom, never light or bold colours. To get the attention on the top, use colours, patterns and texture.

Accessory tips

Necklaces   Choker to medium length will keep the attention near your face.

Brooches   Will be great if you wear them high and towards a shoulder rather than on the lapel. This will bring the eye 'out' and make your shoulders look wider.

Scarves   Best when worn in some horizontal configuration across the shoulders. If you worry about it slipping, secure with a brooch.

Belts   If your waist is worth defining, go for it. Opt for neutral colours that team in with your skirts and trousers.

Shoes   As you will want your hosiery always to be mid-tone to dark to blend with your skirts, choose styles that keep the line of your leg long and lean. Hence, avoid heavy straps or buckles. Matt leathers and suedes will be more effective than shiny materials.

Handbags   If you want your hips to look slimmer, avoid shoulder bags that end in that region. Hand or clutch bags might not be as functional, but will look nicer.

THE APPLE SHAPE

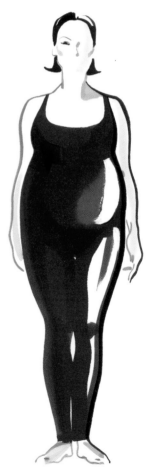

Apple Shape

Famous Examples   Roseanne Barr, Dawn French

You carry all your weight from the shoulders to the hips. From front and side perspective, you have a rounded torso which begins with curved shoulders and a rounded back. Most Apple shapes have little waist area which is compounded to be the centre for their weight accumulation. Often the bustline and waistline almost 'connect', seemingly the same circumference.

But, the big plus for the majority of Apple shapes is their legs, which are often long, lean and shapely. So, if your legs are worth showing, no opaque tights for you, woman!

Choices Are Limited

You will start to have fun with fashion as soon as you come to terms with the limitations of styles you can look great in. That is not a contradiction in terms. Yes, you can look fashionable and current while always selecting the same basic shapes. The key will be to make sure they look new – changing the colours and textures, and accessorising them well.

Jackets

There are plenty of styles in your size, but ignore them all except the long, straight 'cardigan'-style jacket, single breasted and collarless. In these jackets you will look elegant and leaner. When you carry the length to just above your knee or skirt, you can include some pockets for detail as you don't have heavy thighs.

41

Keep it easy and long on top.

When buttoned you want to be able to move freely in the jacket. If you can't, go for the next size up or try a different fabric. As you often have a full bustline, check the positioning of the buttons and be sure there isn't one in line with the nipple as it will make your breasts seem even larger. Buttoning above and below your fullest point of the bust is your most flattering.

Low or collarless styles are preferable to high, wide or fussy collars which only make your neck appear fuller and shorter.

Skirts

Straight skirts on elasticated waists give you the comfort you want, yet make the most of your trim legs. With a short, full waist, you won't wear skirts without an overblouse, cardigan or jacket.

Short lengths will be more slimming than longer ones, but do wear long lengths for variety, and especially if you are average to tall in height. Keep the longer skirt narrow. For example, a long wrap skirt or a simple straight one with a dramatic slit will be great choices for evening. Good pleats for you are narrow knife pleats in an easy fabric that move when you do, but provide a straight line when you stand still.

It's best to avoid very full skirts, tiered or A-line designs which obscure your slim lower half, making you appear full from the neck to your ankles. Another variation of the skirt that is flattering on you is the 'skort', the cross between a skirt and shorts. If the fabric is soft, you can combine comfort with fun, especially for casual wear. Just watch that there isn't too much gathering or excess of fabric which you don't need.

Trousers

You will have more options than other women with curvier hips and fuller bottoms as essentially you are flat on the bottom and hips. Get the comfort you require at the waist, then let the trousers drape into a simple straight line. Leggings or ski-pants when teamed with a fun overblouse or large jumper are also great on you.

Trousers that narrow slightly towards the hem can be elongating on your shape. Fuller styles are possible if you stop short of the exaggerated palazzos or flares.

Dresses

You will find simple, loose designs without any fuss at the waist. Be ruthless about how any dress looks when worn alone. If your shape is too exposed, i.e. if it is obvious that you are wide in the middle due to the cut, then team the dress with a long top. Two-piece knit dresses are nice if the top is loose and long and the skirt very simple.

Colours and Patterns

The most effective way to wear colour with your shape is to keep the top and bottom the same colour, preferably a medium to dark shade, of colours good for you (see Chapter Six). Then your overblouse or jacket can be bright, light or patterned.

Don't be shy with fabric. If the shapes of the clothes are going to be simple, treat yourself to some lovely patterns and fabrics. It's texture that you need to avoid: too much fluff (like mohair), or contrived details like beading and appliqué, will make you look bigger.

For evening, consider a crushed velvet top or satin jacket to make the most of your basic trousers and skirts. If you can't find what you want, treat yourself to some wonderful fabric, and find yourself a considerate tailor to whip up what you want. Vogue Patterns provide some lovely basic shapes every season that you can easily adapt. You'll get years and years of wear and enjoyment out of a special top that you know is right for you.

Accessory Tips

Necklaces They must always be long. Mix chains or several ropes of pearls together.

Brooches You are full in this region, so can do without the detail unless you have some favourite, subtle ones.

Scarves Oblong scarves worn simply draped around your neck or knotted just below the bust will provide interest and colour to any of your stylish basics.

Belts   Now here's where you save money. You don't need even one!

Shoes   Your legs need showing off. Treat yourself to elegant styles – flat or low heels – in the best quality you can afford.

Handbags   Choose medium, never large or lumpy, shoulder bags that fall low on your hips. The 'under the shoulder' shopper is out as it adds fullness to the bust line. Avoid bum bags and back packs for obvious reasons.

Diamond Shape

THE DIAMOND SHAPE

You carry your weight in the mid to lower regions of the torso. Your shoulders are considerably narrower than your hips. The fullness starts at the waist, expands over the hips, buttocks and thighs, then tapers to the knee.

Fit First

To begin with, look for loose, non-tailored designs. Get the fit right over your middle and bottom then see what can be done to adapt the look to flatter you most. Assume that you will have to make a few minor alterations in some cases, to get the garments just right. If you find a nice pair of jersey trousers that are comfortable at the waist and hips but which are too long and voluminous, ask yourself how they can be tapered and hemmed to make you look your best.

Look for blouses, jackets, waistcoats and sweaters that either drape over your hips and bottom, or are slit at the side for ease of movement. Those side slits should close when you are standing still. If they strain from the start, you should try a larger size.

Shoulderline Details

For you, it will be important to broaden the shoulderline with designs that help to balance your figure. Simple V or round-neck tops when worn alone might make your top half look 'droopy' and over-emphasise the hips and thighs. Try to layer simple T-tops with overblouses that have wide collars and/or peaked lapels which still add a bit of detail to make your shoulders appear wider. Yes, you want to look *wider* in this one region.

OPPOSITE A jewel of a look for the Diamond Shape – easy, loose and layered from the shoulders to your most flattering point on the leg.

As with the Pear shape, shoulder pads are your friends for life. Experiment with getting the best fit and shape by trying available options in the haberdashery departments from leading stores. But

beware of layering too many pads (in your underwear, blouses, jackets and coats) with the end result that your neck 'disappears' altogether!

Jackets

In jackets and waistcoats, you know that single-breasted designs are best. Avoid any pockets over the hips as they will only make them appear larger. But a breast pocket, to which you might add a colourful scarf or brooch for interest, would be fine.

Get the length of the jacket perfect. Anything too short or that ends just where you are widest will be unflattering. Your best jacket choice will be the cardigan-style in tightly woven knits, double knits or jersey that will drape your figure and look both becoming and comfortable.

Skirts

The Diamond body shape often has lovely legs, particularly below the knee. As you carry most of your weight in your bottom and thighs, you'll always prefer skirts that end just below the knee, especially if you are short. In longer lengths, be sure to show a bit of ankle, ending the hem just below mid-calf.

Trousers

Your only option will be elasticated waists with styles providing ample room in the bottom and thighs. Better to choose a size or two larger to have the comfort in the waist and hips. If the legs are too voluminous (and too long, no doubt) you'll have to taper and shorten them for best effect. This is an easy job for a local tailor/dry cleaner.

Dresses

Bell-shaped shifts that almost follow your shape will be your most flattering style in a dress. If the design is too straight you will have too much extra fabric in the top half simply to get the fit you require in the middle. Beware of A-line styles, even though they might fit, as the width at the hem will not be as flattering as more tapered styles.

The hem of your dresses should end at an attractive point on your leg. Move around in the proposed length to be sure it is long enough to cover from your knees upwards when you are in motion. And never rely on marking the hem at one point and assuming that you need the same amount taken up all the way round. Because of your shape you need to

COATS

- Go for fit first. Be sure you can button up with ease allowing for extra layers underneath.

- Make sure you can move your arms easily and there is no pulling either over the biceps or across the back.

- Single-breasted designs are more slimming.

- Brighten up any neutral-coloured coat with a bright shawl.

- Use a dramatic brooch to draw attention upwards.

- Tie belted designs at the back not at the waist in front.

- Three-quarter lengths are best for sporty wear/casual lifestyles.

- Avoid the 'Michelin Man' effect – don't wear downy parkas unless you want to look twice your size.

- Macintoshes or raincoats with removeable linings are versatile for wet or cold winter days.

- Complete your look with nice gloves, an attractive yet practical hat or smart, knee-high boots.

- If you hate the restrictions of a coat, and love the cold weather, try a large woollen wrap worn over your jackets as your extra layer instead.

Short jackets aren't necessarily winners on short women. Too much texture and bulk will make you appear wider and shorter.

Minimal bulk in a larger length (and great colour) showing enough leg is a better bet for the shorter women.

pay careful attention to getting the length perfect from front, side and rear.

Colours and Patterns

Your blouses and tops should be in your most flattering colours. Create top interest with lighter and brighter colours, bold prints – even horizontal stripes – for more balance. Stick to plain colours in mid to dark neutrals in your trousers and skirts.

Accessory Tips

Necklaces   Use a choker (unless your neck is short or wide), or medium-length necklaces (18–30 in/45–75 cm long) to bring the eye to your neckline. Long chains just serve to bring the eye to your wider regions where the details of the necklace can get lost anyway.

Brooches   Try a brooch on your lapel when you wear a jacket to bring the attention upwards.

Scarves   Avoid scarves at the neck, but consider large colourful shawls to drape across the shoulders.

Belts   As defined, waisted styles aren't your most flattering or comfortable, so belts won't feature in your wardrobe.

Shoes   Indulge in shoes that show off your ankles. Avoid chunky, strappy styles in favour of ones that are cut long and narrow, showing as much of your foot as possible. No narrow heels or flats. You need a lift in your shoes to create a longer line in your leg but do so with heels no higher than $1\frac{1}{2}$–2 in (4–5 cm). Avoid boots and trainers unless you are wearing them for an appropriate activity.

Handbags   Shoulder bags only serve to make your thighs look thicker. Who needs that? Stick to hand or clutch bags.

CHAPTER 3

LITTLE BUT LARGE

Any woman who is both short and a larger size knows that looking her best is not always a matter of choice. Although gains are being made in every country, with fashions in more sizes, the person with the fewest options for clothes is she who is under 5ft 4in (1.6 m) and size 16 plus (12/14 USA and Canada).

The problem for some manufacturers is that to get the proportions right for the shorter woman who is also a larger size is not straightforward, and can cause real problems with cost-effectiveness when mass-producing a range. In America, where there is a significant 'little but large' market, there are several speciality ranges available at discount as well as designer prices. Gradually some of these lines, as well as additional ones from Britain and other countries, are filtering on to our high streets (see the Resource Directory on page 171). But progress is slow, and the majority of women who are short but a larger size have to make do with ill-fitted clothes designed for taller women.

'Do-it-Yourself' Disasters

For little but large women the challenge becomes finding clothes that cover us, i.e. fit properly over our widest bits, then adjusting the fit as best we can. This generally means buying a jacket and taking the sleeves up, or shortening a hem on a skirt or dress. But, as we discover, a snip here or a chop there may not be all that's required. For even when you get the lengths right for your legs and arms the overall proportions of an outfit can be all wrong and, despite our best efforts and not insignificant investment, we still end up looking like a toadstool!

Most plus or super sizes are designed for the average to taller woman

Standard sizes can be a nightmare for the shorter woman. Here are two women who take the same 'size'. But look how different the same suit looks on the shorter woman (RIGHT). Even after shortening the sleeves and skirt hem, the effect will not be as successful as it is for a woman of average height (LEFT).

with details in scale for *their* bodies, not for shorter women. Hence, breast pockets can end up hovering around the waist, and hip pockets are often mid-thigh on a shorter woman. Interesting and expensive detailing on cuffs or hemlines are lost, as these are the areas which invariably swamp the petite woman, and are subjected to the chop.

When left with no alternative in finding clothes in varying lengths, shorter women have to learn which styling details are possible to alter with some judicious tailoring, and which are hazardous, unlikely ever to be put or look right, and therefore bad investments. Here are a few tips for scaling down fashion to suit your size.

What to Look For

Jackets

- Single-breasted designs will always be easier to put right than double-breasted designs, and will help to make you appear taller. So long as the length is flattering, you can change buttons (if desirable) and/or alter the sleeves to make it work.

- Avoid patch or flap pockets or any detailing on the hips.

- Change excessively large buttons for medium-size ones (you'll need to narrow the button holes). Replace shiny metal ones for buttons with a matt finish.

- Collarless or lapel-less jackets are less risky as lapels can often be so wide or pronounced that they appear to overwhelm you. This will vary with fashion trends. So if you find modestly sized lapels, say in a shawl collar, the jacket might make a nice change.

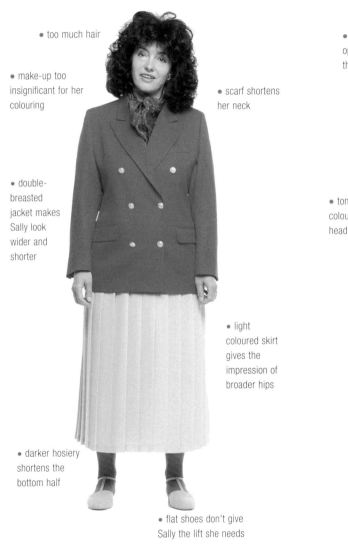

- too much hair

- make-up too insignificant for her colouring

- scarf shortens her neck

- double-breasted jacket makes Sally look wider and shorter

- less hair opens up the face

- an open neckline is more flattering

- toning colours head to toe

- a more slimming single-breasted jacket

- light coloured skirt gives the impression of broader hips

- darker hosiery shortens the bottom half

- flat shoes don't give Sally the lift she needs

- a heel that lifts

Sally before her make over

Here she makes the most of her stature

- Epaulettes or shoulder detailing can be excessive on a shorter woman. If such details can be easily removed, the jacket might be worth considering.

- If the sleeves are very long as well as quite wide, consider tapering them slightly down the forearm. Wide sleeves only serve to make you look fuller and shorter.

- Cuff detailing is best limited to a *few* buttons. Consider replacing the ones that come with the jacket with more interesting ones found in a specialist haberdashery or button shop.

- Avoid contrasting colours on the cuffs.

- On length, consider how versatile the jacket must be, i.e. do you want to wear it with both skirts and trousers. If the answer is 'yes', don't choose a very long style (beyond mid-thigh) as you will look dwarfed in it with trousers.

  If your bottom and hips aren't too pronounced (in reality, not in your imagination), select a jacket that finishes on the hip. You will look taller and more proportioned if you wear a shorter jacket over easy-fitting skirts and trousers in darker or toning colours.

You will reduce your stature if you break up your body with different colours, contrasting hosiery and leg-shortening ankle boots.

Look even taller in a matching trouser suit.

- Avoid waisted jackets, e.g. ones with belts or a tie, although a slight tapering at the waist is always flattering.

Blouses

- Less is best when it comes to style, detailing and print. Very large, stiff or high collars are not good generally on shorter women.
- Try bodysuits if your figure allows, and you like the ease of them under jackets or worn as an extra layer under blouses. As most have some degree of lycra in the fabric, the stretch will enable you to get a good fit in width as well as length. If in doubt, go for a little excess in the crotch to have an easier, more flattering fit in the torso.
- Always adjust the sleeve length on your blouses. Or, simply move the button to ensure a tighter fit on your wrist to keep the finish of the sleeve at wrist, not knuckle.
- Avoid cuff detailing like double cuffs, lace or ruffle trims.
- If the length of the blouse is excessive and you plan to wear it tucked into your skirts and trousers, have extra fabric cut off and finished (a good dry-cleaners will do this for you). Wasted fabric under your clothes only adds unwelcome bulk.
- If you are short-waisted, wear simple T-tops (cotton, silk, polyester, etc) over your skirts and trousers but never longer than the hem of your jackets.

Skirts

- First and foremost, get the fit right over your widest points. If it is your waist, make sure you are comfortable with tops tucked in. The excess over the hips can always be tapered if necessary. Excess left at the waist is more of a hassle, but still easily sorted, and you know you always look much better when your hips and bottom don't look ready to burst out of too-tight skirts.
- Consider shortening skirts from either the waistband or the hem. If the latter is interesting or if the skirt has a kick-pleat or back vent, the only option is to shorten the skirt from the waist. Consult a tailor or the manageress of the shop to ensure this is possible before purchasing.
- If the style has buttoning from waist to hem, provide enough material below a button, at a flattering length, when you shorten, so that the button sits on enough material and doesn't look awkward. For best finish, sew the bottom two buttons permanently closed and the hem will look neater.
- Avoid flap or patch pockets.

SELECTING PATTERNS

ABOVE LEFT Large patterns can overwhelm a shorter stature. It's better to select small to medium size patterns, ABOVE RIGHT.

LEFT If short, consider using patterns only on the top half, to draw the eye upwards.

- Keep patterns subtle and wear with a matching top.
- Avoid bright or light colours in your skirts.
- Very short skirts are more flattering when teamed with a larger overblouse or a jacket. A short, cropped top with a short skirt only serves to make you look short and cropped.
- Show some leg in your longer lengths, i.e. hem the skirts just below the calf where it begins to taper into the ankle.
- When shortening straight skirts (when more than 3 in/7.5 cm is necessary) taper in from the sides as well, i.e. you want to avoid square, boxy skirts.
- Very detailed hemlines – pleats, ruffles, contrasting trim, etc – will make you look shorter so avoid or eliminate if possible.

Dresses

- Get the length of the sleeves perfect. If very detailed cuffs, consider shortening sleeves above the cuff (requires taking the cuff off and sewing back on).
- Simple 'shift' styles are easier to amend than fitted or waisted designs which may be proportioned for a taller figure.
- Taper in the skirt from mid-thigh to hemline to make the silhouette taller and leaner.
- Avoid hems that add width: fishtail, styles cut on the bias, or A-line designs.
- If a button-through design (as with your skirts), shorten the length but allow enough fabric for the bottom button to lie flat.
- If your legs are short, in proportion to your torso, avoid drop-waisted dresses.

Trousers

- Classic or narrow-cut (not skin-tight) trousers will be more flattering than very wide, palazzo styles which can make you look shorter.
- Taper the legs slightly when shortening the hems, beginning from the knee if necessary.
- Eliminate any trouser cuffs which will only make you look shorter.

Stylish Accessories

Since all short women of any size know that they look their best if they don't go too wild in the designs and details of their clothes, you should look to your accessories for creating interest and personality. The accessories you choose will depend on your lifestyle, and how much attention you like from other people. Accessories, like colour, can work like a magnet in getting noticed, so proceed with caution if you are in any doubt about handling attention. If not, go for it!

Jewellery

Earrings Consider your current stash of earrings. Take out your favourites. Put on each pair, one at a time, and ask yourself if you think that they compliment your face. Earrings should enhance your face, not overwhelm it, which is easily done when you are short. Do any protrude so much that they make your face look wider than it is? Are some insignificant with your hairstyle? Are others too noticeable and draw more attention than your face?

Recently, big earrings have been given a rest in fashion, which has been great for shorter women. So many of us looked a bit comical in those overscale numbers of the late 1980s. But remember that although you are short, you are still *substantial* because of your size. So, don't opt for very tiny, diminutive earrings which won't be in scale with your body. The best earrings will be medium in size for clip-ons, or lighter in design yet modest in length for dangling styles.

Necklaces Nothing completes an indifferent neckline better than a pretty or striking necklace. So if you feel you aren't having much fun in your tops due to your size and/or shape, here's where you might indulge yourself with a few treats that will bring you great enjoyment.

If your neck is long, chokers are possible. But being shorter, you are more likely to have an average to shorter neck and therefore will be flattered more by medium to longer length necklaces. Beware of very long lengths in your necklaces. If the chains reach your waist, wrap them around once to create a double strand instead. Or with a long set of pearls, tie a knot mid-bosom, to look really chic.

Don't opt for very fine chains, which will look insignificant on you if worn alone. Several strands together or mixed with beads or pearls can be charming against a simple backdrop of a nice top, jacket or dress.

Bracelets To me, the ultimate in femininity is a lovely bracelet. But if you don't have long arms you need to limit the size and number of bracelets you wear at any one time.

Avoid 'cuff' styles or chunky bangles which will make your arms look shorter and your wrists and hands podgy. Try small to medium link bracelets that are slightly loose on the wrist, never tight. Experiment.

Check out a good selection at a department store and try on different styles. See the effect in a full-length mirror to appreciate if the bracelet is a pretty afterthought (best on smaller women) or a bold statement that might be distracting.

Rings If your fingers are long and not too thick, you will have a choice of rings that will only be restricted by your budget and personality. However, if your fingers are short and hands rather chunky, you don't really want to draw extra attention to them with an excessive number of rings or very large designs. Remember the game is all about highlighting your assets and neutralising your less winning features. So, if your hands are not near the top of your asset list, limit your rings to favourite heirlooms, engagement or wedding bands, and wear them only on the ring fingers.

Scarves

Many short women steer clear of scarves after trying and failing to use them to their advantage. Being shorter and larger will not mean going without, only being shrewd in selecting the right ones for you.

Go for colour in your scarves to add some zip to your wonderfully simple wardrobe basics. Ask yourself what colour or colours would be most versatile. If you have lots of dark or mid-tone neutral basics, brighten them up with a favourite colour from your colour palette (see pages 100–111). For a start, select a scarf in a red or mixture of blues to work with black, navy, grey or beige. A chiffon or silk scarf you could wear year-round while a woollen version might be restricted to the wintertime.

When it comes to style, an oblong will be better than a square. An oblong scarf no wider than 8 in (20 cm) – you don't want too much bulk – will create a vertical line and be very flattering, particularly when wearing one colour underneath. Make sure it isn't too long, i.e. below the waist when tied.

Avoid tying scarves snugly around your neck or using a cravat which might make you look shorter and thicker. Keep your neck area open, tying your square scarves just on the cleavage or just below the bust with an oblong shape.

If you have some pretty shawls, they will be best if worn draped over one shoulder rather than across both which creates a horizontal line that will shorten your stature. Avoid using large bulky wraps over your coat. Some colour at the neck, like a scarf underneath your coat, will be more effective.

Hosiery

Hosiery is an important accessory for every short woman whose goal is to look elegant. The right colour, weight and texture on your legs when wearing your skirts and dresses can make your outfits look twice the price you paid for them.

Resist the temptation to wear very light or nude hosiery when you wear bold or dark colours in your outfits. The effect of light legs will be to 'chop yourself up' visually. Always tone the colour of your hosiery with your skirt and shoes. If the shoes are darker than your skirt, tone the hosiery to them. Try to avoid stark differences in shades between your skirts and shoes. For example, navy shoes with a taupe skirt are perfectly acceptable on many women, but you would look longer and leaner if you toned in taupe shoes with taupe hosiery that was also complementary to your skirt. The key is to tone everything from the waist downwards.

The weight and texture of your hosiery will be contingent on the time of year, obviously, but also on the texture of the clothes you are wearing. Even a light opaque looks too heavy with a cotton denim skirt. Likewise, very sheer, dressy hosiery doesn't balance well with woollens.

Also consider the shape of your legs and their condition. Any discoloration is easily camouflaged with medium to deep hose. Equally, unshapely calves are flattered by these rather than light coloured or lightweight hose.

Shoes

Like any stylish woman, you want a shoe wardrobe to complement your clothes. But unlike all other women, you know that the wrong shoes can look ridiculous and ruin your look if not well-chosen.

Some lift in the heel gives all shorter women a bit more confidence. The key is to limit the height of the heel to that which allows you to walk, skip and jitterbug with ease. Nothing is more comical than a short woman trying to fool the world about her height, tottering around in stilettos. In addition, the width of the heel needs to be in proportion to your size: the bigger you are, the more solid the heel should be. Skinny heels are not flattering on most women, especially you!

Watch the height of the instep in the design of the shoe. The more foot you show, the longer your leg will appear. The shape of the toe can also elongate the foot: slightly tapered, pointed styles are more flattering than very round or square shapes.

Boots should be restricted to wear only when there's snow on the ground! They do nothing for you.

Handbags

Here's where you need some discipline. If you like to carry around the equivalent of an overnight bag, you are probably hurting your overall image, for shorter women look even stumpier. (And I'm not talking about the weekly shopping, but when you are trying to look your best!) Instead you are flattered by sleek, not voluminous, shoulder bags or medium-size clutch/hand-held purses. Very tiny handbags won't be the right scale for you, so resist them even for nights out on the town.

Your Crowning Glory

When you are little but large you need to pay special attention to the cut and style of your hair. The wrong cut can do one of two things: it can make you look even larger, or it can make you look even shorter. The key is to create balance.

Being shorter, you will look better (even taller!) if you don't wear your hair very long or very full. Even if you are blessed with luscious locks, you and your hair will be even more glorious if you choose a style that is flattering but modest in scale.

It's easy to look overwhelmed when you are small, simply by having too much hair

Better balance – your hair should frame your face not hide it

Remember to lift the style at the crown rather than wear your hair very flat on the top (which will make you look shorter). If you have long hair, wearing it in a French twist or in a plait started high on the crown can have the same effect of drawing the eye upwards and making you look a bit taller.

Also, avoid a solid fringe straight across the forehead. While striking on many women and a great trick for women with long-shaped faces, it isn't nearly so flattering on short full women.

A Final Word

So, there you have it, a whole chapter full of tips devoted to you – the little but large who's potentially wonderful. Go back to your own wardrobe and decide what items need immediate rescuing to look better. Only invest in alterations on clothes that you enjoy and have a lot of life left in them. The others can be reserved for gardening or passed on to a charity shop.

Consider your grooming as an integral part of the whole look. Are you doing yourself justice? Are your accessories spot-on or a bit past their best? If so, budget for something new that can be worn for various occasions and help to revitalise several elements of the wardrobe.

And finally, is your hairstyle the best for your special stature? If not, play around at home in front of a three-way mirror. Try pinning your hair up, pulling a few wisps down around your face, to get an idea of how you would look with a new style. Remember not to chop too much, for a very short style can be as unflattering as one with too much volume. Tell your hairdresser what you are trying to achieve and give it a go.

The end result of your efforts will be that people will stop noticing your height and size, and only be aware of dynamite *you*!

CHAPTER 4

SMART SHOPPING: FIGURE AND FIT PROBLEMS

Every woman can list in order of sensitivity her most vexing figure problems. Regardless of size and shape, we all have areas of the body which drive us mad because they are less than perfect and can make finding clothes even more difficult.

Many of us have suffered the disappointment of finding a super top, in our best colours and a good length, only to have to reject it because the collar was a disaster on the neck, or the details on the bustline exaggerated an already ample bosom, or the sleeves were too snug on the upper arm and made us look like a sumo wrestler. Worst is when we compromise in shopping for clothes, and buy things despite the fact that they exacerbate our most challenging features.

This book is all about liberating your style whilst being more selective in shopping. Once you follow the guidelines for your shape, and then consider the following practical tips for your specific challenges, you will end up with a wardrobe of endless possibilities that you'll enjoy year after year. Indeed, your clothes can and should be considered as long-term investments that can be adapted to the current fashions with new accessories or minor adjustments to make them look more current.

Getting the Fit Right

Here's where honesty counts. When trying on new possibilities in the stores, or when weighing up the pros and cons of a new choice from a mail-order catalogue, you have to face up to what works and what

The goal is not to try and look smaller than you are, but to look wonderful, regardless of your size

Sure it 'fits', but is it flattering?

doesn't if you want to look your best. What is the point of deluding yourself that something is OK when you are uncomfortable with the cut? Clothes should be perfect, or have the potential to be made perfect, in order for you to invest in them.

Here are my guidelines for judging fit and, therefore, getting the best value for money as well as the most enjoyment from your clothes.

- **The three-way review is all that'll do!**   Don't size up the fit with a one-dimensional twirl in front of a one-way mirror. You need to see yourself from front, side and rear to judge how the cut of your clothes are working on you.

- **Horizontal stripes mean 'up' the size**   If you see pulling across the back, in the form of horizontal lines, the size is too small. Horizontal stripes across the front of your skirt means that the cut is too straight for your shape. Read more about selecting the best skirts for your shape in Chapter Two.

- **Gaping collars must go**   If you need to increase your size to get the fit you require across the bust or back, but end up with a collar that gapes, see what adjustments might be possible to get a more tailored and flattering fit. If there is seemingly too much collar, try a different style.

- **Button up and breathe**   If you can't fill up your lungs without popping your buttons, the jacket, blouse or skirt is too tight. Remember that tight clothes make you look *bigger* and looser clothes make you look *smaller*.

RIGHT Buttons on everything should do up easily. If they don't, get the next size up.

- **Strain is a pain**   If your thighs are chafing from wearing jeans or trousers that are too tight, if the armholes of your jackets prevent a normal range of movement, and if you can't dash across the street with ease, then the fit is all wrong.

Specific Figure Challenges

Now for more clever tips for dealing with your specific figure challenges, read through what to look for and what to avoid to give you more confidence when shopping.

Short Neck

You will make your face and neck look thicker if you don't open up this area, which is short and full. With man-tailored collars, open a few buttons to expose as much of your neck as possible. This V-line of flesh creates the illusion of having a long neck. For even better effect, stand the collar up in the back, pressing the points in the front downwards to exaggerate the V even more.

The V-neck effect is what you want in your blouses and tops. Even simple round necklines that show some of the neck aren't as effective, especially if your face is round and full. If you have many tops like these that you need to get more use from, mitigate the effect by adding an oblong scarf (tied low) or long chains or ropes of stones or pearls.

With a short, full neck it is more flattering to have a short hairstyle or to wear your hair up. If you have long, shoulder-length or a full hairstyle, your neck will appear even thicker and shorter. See for yourself by using a two-way mirror. Pin your hair up in a knot high at the back of your head and see how much slimmer and longer the neck area appears. If the thought of a shorter style fills you with horror, try a layered style that is tapered at the sides but soft and full at the back with some wisps showing at the neck. You don't want a severely short style, being big, as you will only look larger and less feminine than you are.

What to avoid

- Cowl or turtle necks
- Round peter pan or stand-up collars
- Scarves worn knotted at the neck or as cravats
- Choker necklaces
- Padded shoulders (make your neck appear shorter)
- Epaulettes (broaden the shoulder and neck)
- Coats with thick or high collars
- Round or large earrings that protrude
- Long, dangling styles that are too heavy for your neck

Long Necks

Your long neck is viewed by many as a wonderful asset but to you is often difficult to work into your overall look. The key is to strike a balance between your hair and your necklines.

You need a medium to shoulder length hairstyle to compliment your long neck. Very long, especially straight, styles aren't as good, and short ones need to be avoided at all costs as they only expose what you are trying to soften. Life won't be as easy as it can be with short hair, but just think of how much lovelier you will look!

Now you need to fill up the space created by your long neck. Simple, high necklines aren't always enough, especially if snug-fitting. Try your turtle and cowl necks underneath your blouses rather than wearing them on their own. Stand-up collars of all types are your best, so with your classic man-tailored shirts, prop them up for best effect.

When it's too warm, or you just don't want to wear a layered look, try a chunky choker inside all your blouses. Triple-stranded pearls are worn by many of my clients with long necks, day and evening, and look wonderful. Scarves, of course, also help to fill in this extra expanse whilst bringing colour and personality to your face.

Your tops should be worn loosely, never snug and set-in, and padded shoulders are more effective at broadening this long, narrow region than raglan or dropped shoulders which can exaggerate your neck. If your shoulders are sloping, you will need shoulder pads all the time, not just to straighten the shoulders but also to help balance your neck.

Round or cowl necks in cotton, jersey, wool or silk will soften any harshness, and will be particularly feminine on you.

For evening, when other women slip into skimpy styles with the minimum at the shoulders and neck, you need to do the reverse. Find a stunning blouse, or a dazzling jacket you can leave on all night, that will flatter your best features without exposing an excess of neck. Large, colourful stiffened chiffon blouses can be tried over an attractive body suit with your evening skirts or pants, and are even effective over a simple dress. If worn open, fill in with a diamanté or pearl choker.

What to Avoid

- Tight-fitting tops worn alone
- V-necklines
- Insignificant designs
- Off-the-shoulder designs
- Skimpy fabrics on the top
- Thin long chains worn alone (fine if added to the layered ideas above)
- Raglan or dropped shoulders

Double Chins

Many women who have double chins are also challenged with short or wide necks. So, the advice above for shorter necks will be relevant for you as well.

The key to working with double chins is to realise that trying to camouflage them often just makes matters worse. So keep the area open to look your best. You can distract the eye from your neck by dusting underneath your chin with a soft bronzing powder. If your neck is light, it will be more noticeable.

Obviously, you can't rely on bronzing powder if you don't also make-up your face. For you, make-up is essential to draw attention from a weighty region to some of your best features. Concentrate on your eyes and be sure to blend your foundation down on to the neck (not so that it will come into contact with your blouses, however). Always wear lipstick, another great distraction. Apply your blusher high on to the cheekbones which will help 'lift' the face, taking the attention away from your chins.

See *What to Avoid* for short necks.

Broad Shoulders

Being broad in the shoulders as well as a large size can make some women appear larger than life. While there is little that can be done about your actual stature, there are several things you can try to minimise the breadth of your presence.

Let's start with fabric. It will be important for you to select fabrics that have body, that aren't too delicate or flimsy. The lighter the fabric and colour, the larger your top half will appear. Also, beware of too much texture in your sweaters and tops. Very fuzzy fabrics, like mohair, or thick knits, like Aran, add bulk to the frame.

The patterns in your fabrics can also help to create balance with your broad shoulders. Vertical stripes or patterns will help narrow your upper half. Even though you are probably large boned, very large patterns will create a daunting impression. Very small patterns will be out of scale with your frame. Your best bets will be average size patterns.

A soft shawl in wonderful colours or interesting patterns draped over one shoulder will soften the line at your shoulder. Shawl collars on jackets as opposed to notched or peaked lapels will also help. But better still will be collarless jackets.

Broad shoulders on a woman can make her appear less feminine than she actually is. Work on other areas to dispel this wrong impression, and enhance your femininity. Wear a soft hairstyle, perhaps with some waves or curls. If you like to wear it up or pulled-back, release a few wisps near the face for softness.

In your jewellery, be dramatic and have some fun. Your large scale demands that you draw attention to yourself, and never try to disappear.

If you like earrings, be sure they are significant. Dinky little studs are lost on a gal like you. Go for interesting brooches that draw the eye inwards from your shoulders.

What to Avoid

- Padded shoulders in anything
- Stiff, stand-up collars
- Wide or sharp lapels
- Tight-fitting tops
- Scarves draped over both shoulders, tied in front
- Horizontal patterns on the top
- Bold colour-blocking on top
- Epaulettes and/or excessive shoulder detail

Droopy or Narrow Shoulders

Narrow shoulders on a large woman serve to draw the attention just where you don't want it – to the lower half where you carry your weight. That's why it is essential to build up the top half, yes, even wearing larger tops than normal to look more balanced.

The structure of your tops should be your first focus. Look for jackets that are well-tailored rather than 'deconstructed'. The comfortable cardigan-style jackets are too droopy on you, alas, and will exaggerate your sloping shoulders even more. Go for defined lapels (peaked or notched and the wider the better) as opposed to shawl collars or collarless designs.

A loosely fitted T-shirt will be more flattering than a figure-hugging bodysuit for teaming with your casual clothes. If you like the comfort of bodysuits, wear them coupled with an oversized blouse to give the illusion of being broader. If your waist is neat, tie the blouse in a knot in the middle for an exaggerated blouson style which makes any top appear bigger. But only try this with lightweight fabrics; done with a bulky or stiff fabric, you may look rather chunky.

Any neckline can work, provided you always add shoulder pads to your tops. But the boat neck is particularly good.

Build up the bust, if need be, by wearing a bra with good support or even some extra padding if needed. Often, narrow shoulders seem worse because a woman is small-chested, or because she isn't wearing a flattering bra.

Shawls worn across the shoulders are very effective at drawing the eye out. Try them over coats or with a simple dress.

OPPOSITE PAGE Broard shoulders are flattered by long, loose tops

Epaulettes or leg o' mutton sleeves give added definition to shoulders that can otherwise appear insignificant.

Shoulder bags can be a real hassle as the bag will bounce along on your hips and be pushed down off your narrow shoulders. If you are a natural type, perhaps a student or at home with children, try a backpack instead of a shoulder bag. Depending upon the load you are carrying, you can sling the backpack up over only one shoulder and keep it secure by holding the strap under your arm. For smarter occasions, a clutch bag should do the job.

What to Avoid
- Tight-fitting tops
- V-necklines
- Shawl collars or collarless jackets
- Fine silk, jersey or cotton in your tops
- Long chains or oblong scarves
- Raglan sleeves

TOP Straining at the bust and in the sleeve is both uncomfortable and will make you look larger than you are.

BELOW A looser fit in your blouse is always more slimming. With short sleeves, make sure they end below the fullest part of your upper arm.

Full Busts

No doubt you have discovered many winning tricks to help disguise your generous bustline. First, you will want to be sure that your bra is properly fitted. If in doubt, see Chapter Five for more tips.

The best advice for any full-busted woman is to keep it simple from the neck to the waist. Starting from your collars you want to get it perfect, if possible. A high collar, especially in a stiff fabric like linen or some cottons, makes the bust appear even fuller. But while a plunging neckline might be slimming, it could get you into trouble! My advice is to stop somewhere in between.

Figure-hugging tops are very sexy but risky. Try an elegant loose fit over the bust so that you don't appear to be bursting at the seams. Details in your collars, above the bust, will bring the eye upwards.

One-piece dresses, provided that you can get the fit right elsewhere, are more flattering on you than separates that 'break-up' the overall look. If you find it difficult getting dresses to fit, go for separates but aim for the colours to match or blend on the top and bottom half. If you wear a light top and dark bottom you can highlight the bust, especially if you are also short-waisted.

CHOOSING A JACKET

When choosing a jacket, consider the length. Is it flattering? Does it end at your widest point (jacket **1**)?

Fit is very important. Be sure all the buttons can be done up and that they allow you to move easily. Ask yourself if details like pockets add bulk or draw attention where you don't need it – like to a big bust or full hips (jacket **2**).

The best jackets are in a great versatitle colour, have an elegant loose fit, and end above or beyond your widest point (jacket **3**).

Belts that are cinched too definitely also exaggerate a full bust. If your waist is a feature, wear belts with little or no detail (especially shiny metal buckles).

Longer length tops in your T-shirts, jackets, sweaters, etc. are more flattering on you. The big overblouse teamed with neat trousers or a simple skirt is always fun and sporty. If you have difficulty in getting a generous enough fit in your tops, try the extra-large shirts in the men's department.

As you often need to buy your jackets considerably bigger to accommodate your bust, and end up with more fabric than the rest of you needs, make sure you make the necessary adjustments to look your best. Have the sleeves altered to end at the wrist. If the shoulders are too wide, ask a good tailor to narrow the jacket a few inches from the collar downwards.

In your skirts, a narrow silhouette will be more flattering when combined with a full bustline. Try easy-fitted skirts that drape the body and lie straight when you stand still.

What to Avoid

- Blouse or jackets with breast pockets
- Excessive details on the front of blouses, like ruffles
- Short sleeves that end above the widest part of your upper arm
- Tight-fitting tops (if bodies, always wear covered)
- Stiff fabrics in blouses
- Fluffy knits in sweaters

No Waist/Big Tummies

For some perfectly proportioned women their only challenge is in having a full waist. Perhaps as a result of childbirth, or because of heredity, they retain all their excess weight in the middle. The effect is a waist that doesn't seem to indent at all, and may indeed protrude.

Your objective is twofold: to wear comfortable waistbands, and to keep the area covered, i.e. with long tops. If you can avoid waisted styles altogether, wearing dresses rather than skirts, for instance, all the better. What you choose will depend on your lifestyle.

In your tops be clever in selecting colours and patterns that won't exaggerate your fullness in the waist. Vertical stripes in blouses and jackets will be especially good. But remember that plain colours are probably better.

Watch the details at the hem of your tops. Make sure there is no strain over the girth and that closings can be fastened easily. Nothing will show off your fullness more than tops that end at your widest point and appear to be stretched to their limit.

Opt for blended fabrics that don't crease as easily as natural fibres. Strained horizontal stretch marks only call attention to where you don't want it. If comfort is a consideration, don't choose totally man-made fibres, but select part natural and artificial blends. Soft fabrics that drape will also be more flattering than stiff alternatives that will gape over your tummy.

Long waistcoats and jackets that finish in a straight or curved inverted V are your best.

What to Avoid

- Double-breasted tops
- Patch or flap pockets on hips
- Bold patterns in your tops
- Knits, except for fine ones
- Short, hip-length designs
- Belts

Short Midriff/Waist

Many of us retain our weight at the waistline which can make fitting into skirts and trousers tricky as well as potentially uncomfortable. One advantage to carrying weight here is that you feel it quickly and thus can cut down on the wrong foods or introduce a bit more exercise to tone up.

A full waist is often made worse when there is little space in the midriff area. You can easily tell if you are short-waisted by looking in a mirror wearing a white top and dark skirt or trousers. Tuck in the top. Do you look squashed in the middle? If you add a belt at the waistline, does it make you look even fuller than you are, principally due to the lack of space? If so, you probably have a short midriff. Don't despair. No-one need know you have this problem if you follow some of our foolproof style tricks. Besides, if you are lacking in space in the waist you are no doubt blessed with longer legs. So, it's not all bad news.

As you have discovered, long tops are your most flattering. The big overblouse, worn loose over your trousers and skirts, looks fabulous and really disguises a short, full midriff. However, if you need to look smart and feel the overblouse is a bit too relaxed, try a simple top tucked into your skirts but pull it down loosely over your waistband to create the illusion of having a longer midriff.

Dresses will be wonderful on you, particularly if you fit easily into one size (as opposed to needing different sizes on the top and bottom). Look for long, easy chemise-style dresses or coat-dresses that aside from some modest tapering have little waist definition.

TOP Short tops in accent colours can exaggerate a full waist

BELOW Longer tops in softer fabrics are always more slimming

A tight fit might be trendy, but will not always be flattering.

If you like belts, wear them in a colour to tone with your tops, not your bottoms, to help bring the waistline down. This works well with your dark tops, but can look a bit unsuccessful in light colours: a white belt with a white blouse is fine in summer for casual wear, but has limited use the rest of the year, and for smarter outfits.

What to Avoid
- Short jackets and fitted tops
- Belted designs in jackets and dresses (in coats, tie the belt loosely at the back)
- Wearing stark colour contrasts on the top and bottom
- Wearing belts unless necessary (try to tone in, not contrast with colour of outfit)
- Tight-fitting tops
- Very gathered waistlines

Low Waist

Here we have an asset as well as a challenge. The plus points of a low waist are that you can wear belts (if you have a nice waist) and can make the most of your tops. The difficulty is in balancing your longer torso with your shorter legs which might also be large.

Your inclination will be to wear long tops to cover the girth. When you do this and wear long skirts or full trousers you will look shorter and wider, not anyone's goal. Find your widest point on the hips or thighs, and finish your tops and jackets above it. Your goal is to make the bottom half look longer than it is, and you achieve this by *shortening* the top half.

With long skirts, you might find that they come up very long on you (ankle-length) in order to accommodate the size needed for your hips. Remember to have a few inches cut off – to end just below mid-calf – so that you look balanced.

Follow the advice above if your hips and bottom are full. If they aren't too bad, you still want to keep it simple with easy designs, and medium to dark colours. Tone your hosiery to the colour of your skirts, and match with the colour of your shoes.

If your legs are nice and you like shorter skirts, combine them with a longer jacket for best effect. The short jacket is best with your long skirts and trousers. With everything – skirts and trousers – you will need shoes with a bit of a heel. Flats will only make your legs look shorter.

What to Avoid

- Very long and full skirts
- Flat shoes
- Long jackets with long skirts
- Overblouses with full trousers
- Hip pockets on jackets and cardigans
- Drop-waist dresses

Heavy Arms

Heavy arms can plague some women who aren't necessarily vastly over-weight. For some of us, we've inherited Auntie Sophie's podgy limbs, and no amount of dieting seems to shift the bulk. As we age, we tend to use full arm extensions less and less, which can cause flabbiness in the slight-est of women. So for bountiful beauties over 35, the problem can really restrict style options, particularly for evening and in the summertime.

The good news is that exercise really does tone fat arms, and you can see the difference quite quickly, say after a month of regular swimming. So, if your arms really drive you mad, do something about them with some arm exercises.

Until your arms are back in the shape you desire them to be, consider the following style tips to minimise their impact. Obviously, long sleeves hide big arms but the key is also to wear loose-fitting sleeves. Tight sleeves call attention to the arms. Keep your blouses and tops easy rather than close-fitting – an exaggerated classically tailored blouse in a good cotton will be better camouflage than a jersey polo which is clingy.

Layering with a waistcoat over your blouses takes the attention away from the arms, while creating some interest with colour and design with-out the full bulk of a regular jacket which can be constricting on some women with big arms. Another trick is to wear an attractive oblong scarf over your blouses which is both slimming as well as balancing to your arms. Long chunky beads will have the same effect.

In the summertime, hunt for diaphanous tops that you can wear over your swimming costume or tank tops with your skirts or trousers. Roll the cuffs up just below the elbow to show off your lovely forearms and make the most of your manicure, bracelets and rings to draw attention where you want it.

What to Avoid

- Short sleeves or sleeveless tops
- Tight-fitting tops
- Thick texture in sweaters and tops
- Boxy, stiff jackets
- Very fine fabrics in blouses

Full Hips/Big Bottoms

Why do features that can be so voluptuous in the flesh be so troublesome to make look wonderful in clothes? Short of running off to a naturist camp, all you need to do is learn how to balance the fullness of your hips with the rest of your body by selecting the right styles and fabrics in your skirts and trousers.

Full hips become an issue when they are more ample in relation to the rest of the body. So the challenge is to make less of them. You achieve this by wearing fabrics that drape rather than fabrics and designs that try to conceal. Stiff, tailored cuts might fit, but they will make your hips appear larger than they actually are. The difference between your hips and waist can cause difficulties, so choose only skirts and trousers with elastication.

Your skirts should be flirty and floaty. When you stand still they shouldn't stick out, i.e. be too voluminous. Hence, jersey, knits, stonewashed silks and microfibres will all be good bets.

Trousers might not work, especially if your bottom really does protrude. If your bottom is ample, but flat, trousers and culottes will be fine. However, if from the side view the indentation at the waist is very striking in comparison to the bottom, your natural assets are best draped over and not highlighted with trousers.

Same style, different fabrics. Soft knife pleats on an elasticated waistband fall straighter and are more slimming, even in an lighter colour (LEFT). Stiffer fabrics, like crinkled microfibre (RIGHT), stand fuller and can make you appear larger.

Wear long tops that go beyond your fullest point and end where you start to taper inwards. This will help to make you look taller and less broad on the beam. But, more important, bring the attention to other parts of the body you might more happily show off – a great bust, wonderful shoulders, terrific ankles, whatever.

Wear darker colours on the bottom half as they will draw less attention to your bottom. But don't play it safe on the top half. This illusion only works if you have fun with colour and design in your blouses, jackets and scarves while neutralising your bottom in dark colours and simple designs.

Big bottoms require substantial shoes to look elegant. Very high heels are ridiculous as well as uncomfortable, and flat shoes will make you look even fuller. Try a slightly raised heel of significant depth, not narrow ones. Court shoes will be very flattering, particularly if they are cut low on the foot, making your feet look even longer and lovelier.

What to Avoid

- Straight skirts
- Tight-fitting trousers and skirts
- Shorts
- Light colours and patterns on the bottom half
- Shiny, flimsy, stiff or bulky fabrics in your trousers and skirts
- Short tops or blouses tucked in
- Chunky belts

Heavy Thighs

There is one consolation (and only one!) in having heavy thighs: you retain your weight in the region considered safest by the health experts. Women who carry their weight in their tummies add worrying strain on their hearts. Full thighs may carry very little health risk, but can be a major problem when trying to look your best.

Many women deal with heavy thighs by assuming a bin-liner mentality – they try to cover themselves head to toe in a large sack-like garment. Lo and behold, where does the strain always show? Right in the cellulite zone, mid-thigh.

You need to follow similar advice to women with full hips and bottoms in as much as you need to keep your skirts and trousers simple and dark. Skirts cover thick thighs more comfortably than trousers, although trousers are fine on women whose thigh problem is not so exaggerated. The skirts, however, should be in substantial material, neither thick nor flimsy. If the fabric is light you need a lining or slip underneath to prevent clinging.

The key to dealing with heavy thighs remains less in the style of skirt and more in your undergarments. If you haven't tried one, I would urge you to experience the wonders of long-line panty girdles or even tights with built-in support from the tummy down through the thighs. These wonder garments can take inches off without any more exertion than needed to get them on (which can't be underestimated). Support will be needed if you like to wear knits or sheer or clingy evening wear. Big thighs are not as bothersome as jiggling thighs.

Trousers or culottes are great options for full thighs if they are not too tailored and drape. The better the fabric the more successful the effect. Just make sure that there is no strain over the thighs. If the cut is too snug, get the next size. If the next size still can't provide a loose fit over the thighs, choose a skirt instead. Nothing makes thighs appear larger than tight trousers. Wrong, shorts *always* do.

What to Avoid

- Straight skirts
- Flimsy or heavy fabric in skirts or trousers
- Light colours or bold patterns on the bottom half
- Shorts
- Low/classic leg cuts in swimsuits
- Going without tights under anything
- High heels or flats
- Heavy shoes like Doc Martins or trainers (except for exercise)
- Leggings and stirrup pants
- Tops that end at mid thigh
- Hip or flap pockets on jackets, cardigans or skirts

Heavy Lower Legs

Heavy or unshapely lower legs present real challenges for many women, often women who aren't generally large. No amount of exercise can help to change the shape, it seems, so minimise the impact of your legs on your overall look through the clothes you wear.

Resorting to a life in trousers is a drastic measure, and unnecessary unless you love trousers. With a friend to give you feedback, stand in front of a mirror and decide on the best length for your skirts. If your calves aren't too large, perhaps just above them is possible. If they are big, your best bet will be to wear those lovely, longer 'tea' length skirts, ending just above the ankle.

The link between the shoes, hosiery and skirt colours is vital. For best effect, to neutralise the impact of your legs, keep your skirts medium to

TROUSERS

1 Elasticated waists are comfortable but excessive gathers can make you appear larger than you are.

2 Classic-cut trousers in stiff fabrics can crease and strain over full curvy figures.

3 Trousers in soft fabrics and with some easy gathers but a flat panel over the tummy are attractive on most women.

dark, with your hosiery toning with the depth of the skirt and your shoes. Unless your legs also suffer from veins or patchy skin, sheer hosiery is fine (especially in the spring and summertime).

What to Avoid

- Short skirts
- Tight leggings
- Straight skirts
- Light colours in dresses and skirts
- Light hosiery and shoes
- Extreme styles in shoes – too clumpy or too flimsy

Big Feet

The main hassle about having large feet is in getting attractive styles in shoes. By now you will have found a few trusty outlets, but you still need to ensure you are selecting complimentary styles.

KNITS

Look fabulous and feel comfortable in wonderful knits. Available in a wide range of colours, at discount as well as designer prices, knits should feature prominently in every modern woman's wardrobe.

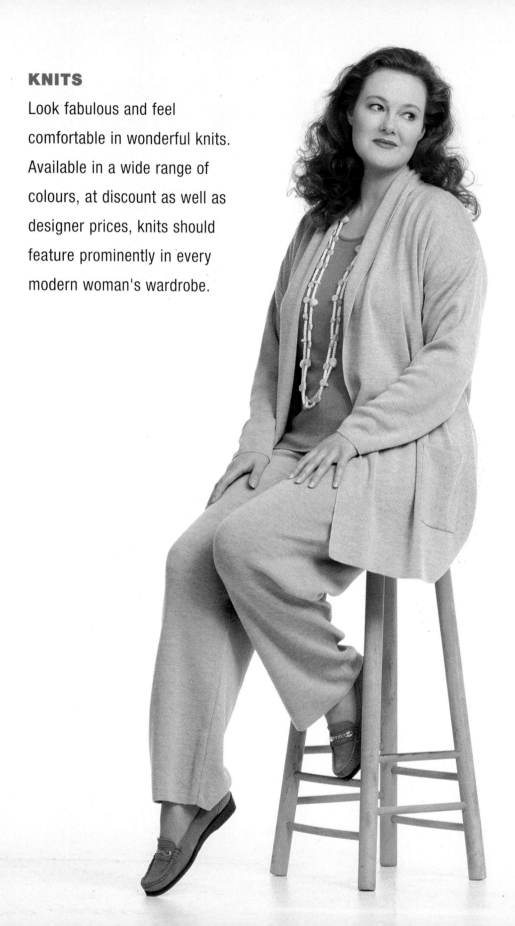

Wide feet are best flattered by simple styles, like court shoes. Lace-up styles, unless necessary for orthopaedic reasons, only exaggerate a full foot. Choose styles that are more pointed than round at the toe. And go for a slight lift in the heel, never more than $1\frac{1}{2}$ in (4 cm), in a solid design (i.e. not stiletto).

What to Avoid

- Delicate styles
- Very high heels
- Excessive detailing like buttons and bows
- Multi-coloured shoes
- Ankle or T-straps

If you have large feet that aren't wide, you can have more fun with styles, provided that they don't make your feet look any larger. Darker colours will succeed better than lighter ones. Men's slip-ons are nice alternatives for casual wear and may be less expensive than special-order female styles.

CHAPTER 5

FIRM FOUNDATIONS

There's little point in spending time planning your wardrobe, and spending money on nice clothes, if you are totally indifferent to what you wear underneath. The foundations of your clothes – your bras, pants, hosiery, etc. – affect the final finish of your overall look.

If in any doubt about the importance of good underwear, treat yourself to a feast of good and bad examples by having a coffee at a sidewalk café and watch what walks by. The summertime is best for this experiment. First, notice the women in the tight bodysuits with lacy bras underneath. They might as well be wearing arrows pointing at their breasts for the effect of the lace under tight or sheer tops is to shout 'Look at us'! There might be women in clinging blouses which reveal bras digging excessively into flesh. All you see are ripples and bulges everywhere. You can also see women with a curious *amount* of breasts. There can't be four? Or is that just one mega-boob, not really two? Bizarrely fitted bras alone could amuse you for hours. Another disaster is the pantyline, so much more prevalent under lightweight fabrics or when ill-fitting knickers are worn alone without the support of tights. Or the bulges at the waist caused from excessively tight panty girdles. The list of possible mishaps is long.

Don't believe what they say. Size matters.

Yes! Big is beautiful, as long as you wear the right size bra with adequate support.

Are Your Foundations Letting You Down?

To see how well you prepare your image from the foundations, take the following quiz. Circle the answer that best applies to you.

	Yes	No
1. I have been properly measured for my bra size within the last three years.	☐	☐
2. I have different styles and colours of bras to work with the various fabrics and necklines that I wear.	☐	☐
3. I only buy new panties when I am down to my last pair.	☐	☐
4. I wear sexy underwear because it makes me feel feminine all day long.	☐	☐
5. In the summertime, it is too hot for tights so I always go without.	☐	☐
6. Underslips aren't necessary and are a useless purchase.	☐	☐
7. My man hates large cotton panties so I only wear silk bikini styles.	☐	☐
8. My tummy isn't firm, so I wear tights rather than stockings.	☐	☐
9. My main concern is with the fit of a swimming costume, not necessarily the design of it.	☐	☐
10. Girdles are for grannies!	☐	☐

Answers

1. **Yes** If you haven't been measured for the correct size bra by an expert, you are probably wearing the wrong size. If you are wearing the wrong size you aren't making the most of your figure. See pages 85–6 for more guidelines on getting the right size and style bra for you.

2. **Yes** Well done. You know the importance of the right colour bra as well as the right fit under your tops.

3. **No** Your undies should be replenished at least twice a year providing you have a good stock to keep up with wear and frequency of washing. When you pick up a couple of new pairs, edit the same number of worn ones and relegate as dusters. Don't leave worn, stretched-out knickers to clutter your drawers. Chances are you'll still wear them and not be looking your best.

4. **No** Sexy underwear is best worn on its own rather than as underclothes. The provocative designs and flimsy construction of most of this type of underwear leave you jiggling and bouncing all day long. By the end of the day in sexy undies, you'll probably feel worn out rather than in the mood!

5. **Yes and No** In the summertime, when relaxing with friends or on holiday, the last thing you want is to bind yourself in lycra. But for work or a dressy occasion you should wear some form of hosiery. There are plenty of options to make you look polished as well as feel comfortable with hosiery in the summertime. See page 88 for more details.

6. **No** Underslips can make some inexpensive skirts and dresses look twice what you paid for them by helping them drape better. And, nothing reveals the size of your thighs better than a clinging skirt.

7. **No** If your man doesn't like full cotton panties, he doesn't have to wear them! What you choose to wear under your clothes all day long should be up to *you*, knowing what is most comfortable and makes you look well-groomed. Change into whatever you and he prefer for intimacy when you get home.

8. **Yes** Indeed, tights are wonderful for holding in all the jiggles, especially if you like to wear fitted styles. Save the stockings for when you wear full skirts and longer lengths.

9. **Yes and No** The fit of your swimming costume is important, but so is the design. Don't stop just when you get the fit right. Ask yourself if the colour and design are flattering. If not, soldier on and find a better alternative. A well-chosen costume, if taken care of, can last and be enjoyed for years. See pages 89–90 for more details.

10. **No** Although many older women favour a 'corseted' look rather than letting everything hang loose, there are some wonderful new alternatives to the old-fashioned girdle for women of all ages, sizes and shapes. See page 87 for more details.

Slinky camisoles when worn without a bra are best reserved for the bedroom

Bras

Selecting the right bra isn't as straightforward as it seems. Sure, they are generally displayed according to size and style, but variations in both design and manufacturer may produce a different fit. Have you ever rushed into a department store and grabbed what you thought was pretty much a copy of your favourite bra, in the right size, only to get it home and to find yourself squirming because it doesn't fit?

To choose the right bra first takes an analysis of how well your current stock is working for you, and then learning your correct size and style options to link with your wardrobe.

Sorting Out Your Bra Wardrobe

Dig into your drawers and pull out all your bras. Did you realise you had so many? What is it about bras? When we buy new ones we never throw the old ones away, we hang on to them 'just in case'. But with newer ones in better condition, we never wear the old ones, and have to plough through them every day to find the fresher models. So, why not toss out those relics today, then look and see what's left and in a wearable state.

Now separate the comfortable bras from the ones that dig or sag and are a bore to wear. Check the size and style of the ill-fitting ones. Are they the same as your better bras? If not, what's different? Even though some of the bras may hardly have been worn, it is no use cluttering your undie drawer with them. Put them aside, and plan to give them away to a charity shop.

Now put on the bras that you think are a good fit. Does the back of the bra ride up and the cups sag? If so, the bra is too small and the design is wrong for you. Do you fill the cup, or are there wrinkles? If so, the cup size is too big. Are you bursting out of the bra, over the top? If full-busted and brimming over the top of your bras, you will look 'four-breasted' in your clothes. You need a large cup size. The 'wonderbra' effect is only for the small-chested.

Confused? You are not alone. If you have been wearing the same size bra for the last five to ten years, you are probably wearing the wrong size. As our body shapes can fluctuate, so too can our bust size and shape. The elasticity of the bust can alter dramatically with dieting, pregnancy, breast-feeding, and with ageing. Pert breasts that once seemed to defy gravity can change within a year and require a new size and style bra to look their best.

Research done by Britain's largest lingerie retailer, Marks & Spencer, reported that most women who wear a dress size over 14 (10/12 USA and Canada) preferred non-wired bras even though they were the ones who needed them most. They also found out that the majority were wearing the wrong size, bras that were invariably too small.

THREE TYPES OF BUSTS

Average   Breasts that require some help to achieve shape. If unsupported will look flatter than they are.

Firm   More 'elastic' and pert. Have most choice in styles to wear. Generally, but not always, younger breasts.

Soft   Needs proper construction to shape the breast. Without a bra, these breasts sink or sag.

If full-busted you also may have had trouble with traditional under-wiring in bras, as they can dig into the flesh and be quite painful to wear for a full day. Women who carry particularly heavy breasts bear the added discomfort of sore shoulders where the straps dig into the flesh from carrying the extra weight of the breasts.

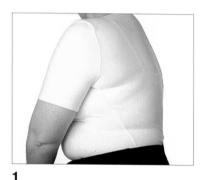

1

2

3

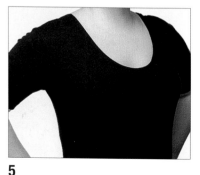

4   **5**

1 The wrong bra is both uncomfortable as well as unflattering.   2 The 'mattronly loaf' is caused by wearing either a cup too small or a style without adequate support.   3 The wrong sized bra can be disastrous. Is that four I see?   4 Be sure the colour and design of your bras are appropriate for your tops.   5 Your best bra makes the most of your shape, and is more slimming.

The Right Support Bra

Traditional bras, no matter how accommodating the size, don't meet the needs of the generously endowed. You have to seek out specialist ranges which, thankfully, are becoming more and more accessible on our high streets and via mail order (see our Resource Directory at the end for details). Proper support means an ample cup size to carry your load, but also extra padding and width in the shoulder straps to be gentler on the skin. The style should always include underwiring and be well-designed to 'lift and separate' the breasts to give you a nice, feminine shape. A bra that simply holds everything together, into one great matronly loaf, does no woman's figure any favours.

HOW TO MEASURE YOURSELF

Step one Measure your chest under your arms for your *bra size*.

Step two Measure the fullest part of your bust for your *cup size*.

If your cup size is:

Up to 2 in (5 cm) larger than your bra size, you need a B cup

Up to 3 in (7.5 cm) larger, you need a C cup

Up to 4 in (10 cm) larger, you need a D cup

Up to 5 in (12.5 cm) larger, you need a DD cup

Up to 6 in (15 cm) larger, you need an E cup

Up to 7 in (18 cm) larger, you need an F cup

Up to 8 in (20 cm) larger, you need a G cup

Up to 9 in (23 cm) larger, you need an H cup

Up to 10 in (25.5 cm) larger, you need an I cup

The only way to determine whether a bra meets your needs is to try one on. But don't rely on your own judgement. Get an expert's advice at a specialist shop or store who can tell you if the bra does the job properly. If successful, invest in three bras at a time (in different colours), and make a note of the style and size for when you need to replace them.

Get an Expert Opinion

After measuring yourself at home, and realising that you are probably wearing the wrong bra size, the next step is to consult an expert. You should be re-measured by a specialist bra-fitter every three to five years or even every year if you have had a baby or changed in weight (as little as 10–12 lb or about 5 kg can make a difference).

Although the fitter might confirm your measurement (after using the guidelines above) appreciate that the inches or centimetres are only the starting point. As women all vary in shape, an expert eye will know what style as well as size might be best for you. Tell the fitter what you want to achieve as well as the sort of necklines, fabrics and clothes you wear. Snug-fitting bodies and knits require a smoother finish than looser blouses. Lower necklines and backless, strapless clothes need their own special foundations. And don't be shy about mentioning your desire to look sexy, if that's what you want for special dresses or occasions. A trained sales adviser should give you daytime and evening options.

Colour Coordination

Although available in every colour under the sun, women only need two colours in their bras to go with most of their wardrobe: white or ivory bras to wear under white and pastel tops; and a black bra for wearing under rich and deep colours. How wild you go otherwise is down to your personality and budget.

Panties

Unlike your bras, you can select your knickers yourself and don't need an expert to tell you which are winners and which let you down. You've discovered that through trial and error on your own.

Scoop 'em all out of your undie drawer and eliminate those that are well past it, with overstretched waistbands, ripped lace, discoloration, etc. Out of what's left, which styles can you wear under your trousers with comfort? If you wear trousers often, do you have enough of this style to meet your needs? Nothing is more annoying than knickers that ride up your bottom. The best fit for trousers is the full brief that provides ample, comfortable coverage of your entire bottom. Indeed, these are not your sexy numbers, but they do the job best.

G-string panties are for gals with toned bottoms and who don't mind the feeling of having their buns 'flossed' all day. You don't have to worry about visible pantyline, but if your bottom jiggles it's just as bad.

Under snug-fitting skirts and dresses you are advised to wear slightly looser rather than tight-fitting panties. Best are the high-waisted versions which prevent the bikini line which is so often on view. Yes, these can look sweet, especially with high cut legs. But be sure you get ample bottom coverage. Avoid panties that have detailing, on the leg especially, which might be revealed under your clothes.

'Tap pants' or silk shorts are cute for romping around the house but provide a unsuccessful base under your clothes as they invariably ride up and cause bulges. Obviously, you need to take the greatest of care in the fit of your panties under neat-fitting items. Under loose dresses and skirts, whatever is comfortable is fine.

Control panties – brief and longline – can work wonders as well as make you feel miserable. Here's another area where expert advice should be sought. If you like the feeling of being held together, and you don't want to be constantly sucking your tummy in yourself, you might like the feel of control panties. If you've never worn them, start off with a style with minimal control. See how long you can wear them and feel comfortable.

G-strings (TOP) may look fab on their own but can cause havoc under snug-fitting clothes. Reserve them for romping around in at home, unless your thighs and buns are toned.

Good fitting knickers (SECOND PICTURE) never dig into the flesh.

The 'total control' panties can take inches off your body but can also inhibit natural movement as you feel as though you are in a strait-jacket. I once wore a combination control slip and panty number under a skirt in the days when skirts were short and tight and a nightmare. Every time I leapt forward with one leg, the other one would involuntarily snap in behind. When I was dashing for a taxi, I felt as though I was being catapulted down the street in a rubber slingshot! The other disadvantage to wearing very tight control panties or girdles is that they restrict circulation and normal muscle movement which isn't good for any of us on a daily basis. So, perhaps these magical panties which make us look slimmer and firmer than we are are best reserved for special occasions, when you've just got to fit into that damn dress!

Tell-tale Bodies

Bodysuits are now available in larger sizes and a favourite for all women who like to look pulled-together with the minimum of fuss. But the bodysuit adds an extra leg-line under your clothes and is often constructed with stronger elastic and seams which are more distinguishable under skirts and trousers than your knickers.

To prevent the dreaded 'pantyline' in your bodies, wear them without panties and underneath your tights. Yes, under not over. The effect of the tights over the body base is to smooth down the leg line. It works a treat. Try it.

All-in-One Undies

For those special occasions when you need to undress in 'company', consider an all-in-one bodysuit that is your bra and panties combined. There are plenty of lacy, colourful, feminine designs that can keep you 'all-together' and lovely when you need to impress someone special.

All-in-one undies, however, provide minimal support, so they aren't a certain choice under everything. If you need reliable control and shaping in your bra, you won't get it in these bodies. Or, if you are wearing a slinky dress you might not have as definable a shape as you would like in an all-in-one. So experiment before investing.

All-in-one underwear can be both comfortable and effective under tighter fitting clothes. Opt for a slightly larger rather than smaller size, for best results.

Hosiery

Simply put, get the right fit for you. Queen or extra-large sizes fit body shapes and heights differently. So, it's down to you to discover which brand caters best for your body. Don't throw the packaging away when you buy your tights. Keep it for a day. If you like the fit, make a note of the brand, size and colour as tights are rarely labelled themselves.

If you carry your weight in your tummy, beware of excessive control-top tights which can be so constricting that they force your weight up and over your waistband. However, for manageable bulges some amount of extra control can be a welcome bit of support, especially when wearing just one layer, i.e. going without a jacket.

For women who have their excess weight in their hips and thighs, control top and extra thigh support in their tights can be magic. If you haven't tried these tights before, experiment with one pair. Err on the side of the tights being a larger size than you might need. They will still shape to your body, and you can determine if the amount of support is comfortable or if you can take more (perhaps, by wearing your accurate size).

In summertime when hosiery isn't necessary (for play, on holiday, etc.) you might suffer from chafing thighs. No amount of vaseline seems to help on a hot sticky day if your thighs constantly rub together. A good remedy is to wear cotton cycling or aerobics shorts under your floaty dresses and skirts as well as T-shirts and tops. They will keep your thighs firm, separate and the chafing to a minimum. Dust the inside of the shorts with some talcum powder before putting them on to help absorb some of the extra sweat.

Swimsuits

Most of us love a holiday in the sun, and welcome the chance to soak up those warm rays (with the protection of ample sunfilters, of course). The last thing we want to worry about is our swimsuit – will it be comfortable, will it be flattering?

The following guidelines will help show off your best assets when you select your next swimsuit.

A great swimsuit is both flattering and comfortable

How to Choose the Best One for You

For slimmer thighs Choose a high-cut design. Vertical stripes or dark side panels help to elongate your body and bring the eye up from the thighs.

For making the most of your bust Choose a style that has detail at the bust line, either a lighter panel, a bow or horizontal stripes. If you team with a deeper colour on the bottom the bust becomes even more prominent.

For minimising the bust Select a style with no colour or styling details at the bust. If you can get away without a formed cup, so much the better. But only opt for these unstructured styles if there is an inner panel to hold the bust in place, not allowing it to slide towards the midriff.

To flatten your stomach A skirted style is best along with a fabric and design that helps to pull the tummy in. Diagonal stripes draw the eye away from the stomach.

To 'create' a narrow waist Select styles with belts or panels at the waist. Sometimes just a few vertical stripes at the waist will do the trick.

CHAPTER 6

Colour counsel

I hope you need little convincing about the wonders of colour. Think about how you feel when you wear certain colours. Are you aware of the different reactions you get when you wear bright colours as opposed to soft colours? Do you have colour biases, or restrict the use of colour because of your size?

Even discussing colours with some bigger women forces them to become defensive. Most have been conditioned to believe – falsely – that if they wear black they will look much thinner and slimmer. The retailers perpetuate this myth by offering the bulk of their *plus* or *super* sizes in this funereal colour or its closest cousin, navy blue. Other women state that they would give anything for more colourful choices in their wardrobes, but the designers are all bent on trying to make bigger women *disappear* in dark and dreary clothes.

It has been the rare client over a size 16 (12/14 USA and Canada) who feels she can be experimental in wearing colours. The majority tell me, 'Oh, no! I just couldn't be that adventurous.' But when colours are well-selected for the woman herself, and she is given a range of options in her wardrobe, she is in control of the impact she wants to make on others in her life. Yes, colour gives you power. It helps tell the world what kind of a woman you are and helps you achieve your objectives.

Grace's Story

Grace is a woman you never forget. She is a raven-haired 6 footer (1.83 metres tall), and a size 22 (18/20 USA and Canada). A former opera-singer, now motivational trainer, Grace came to me because she was increasingly frustrated in her marketing efforts. She was convinced her image was part of the problem. Her business was thriving mainly due to

Wearing the right colours affects your self-image as well as how people respond to you.

BEFORE

AFTER

personal recommendations. But to really succeed, she needed to win a few bigger clients, and this involved some targeted cold-calling on companies who regularly used trainers such as herself, but for whom she had never worked.

'I wow them over the telephone. They are eating out of my hand, sight-unseen,' explains Grace. 'Then comes the first meeting and *wham!* As soon as I enter the meeting I see their faces drop and they practically run for cover.'

Well, I nearly did the same on my first encounter with Grace. Being only 5ft 3in (1.6 metres), and half her size, I too was overwhelmed by this human dynamo. Grace had had her colours done by a CMB consultant and now dressed exclusively in her Autumn colours – wonderful warm tones of moss, bronze, chocolate brown, aubergine, golden yellow and tomato red, to name just a few. But like many newly colour-analysed women, Grace went for her colours without considering the effect they had on others.

One of her first purchases in her new colours while on business in Munich was a pumpkin-coloured suit. Sure, it was technically a wonderful colour on her, and although not out of place that season in Germany, she looked like she'd landed from another planet when she tried to market herself in it in the North of England. I could just imagine them backing away in Newcastle! Grace had to learn a thing or two about using colour more effectively, and to consider the impact of colours in relation to her height, size and *her* outgoing personality.

First we had to analyse the role Grace was performing. She was selling herself. To do that she needed to convince these prospects that she could solve their problems, and meet their needs of motivating their staff into being more productive. Too often women, and men for that matter, mistake the selling role as one in which you need to impress. This can get wrongly interpreted, and becomes one in which you make too strong an impact. Effective selling requires an image that looks successful, but does not overwhelm. You need to develop an image that enhances your ability to build rapport with others.

My advice to Grace was to reserve the pumpkin number for when she had to give a presentation to an audience of no less than 500, and to find a more neutral suit in one of her Autumn colours. Bold colours help to hold the attention of a large audience, but can have the opposite effect, that of overpowering a small gathering.

Fortunately, chocolate brown had just been launched as the new fashion neutral of the season, and it was a winner on Grace. But because of her personality, Grace needed to add a bit more excitement to the basic brown suit – this was a woman who hated anything drab. Rather than endorse her choice of a boldly patterned blouse, I convinced her that a colourful, tonal scarf in warm greens, worn with a basic cream bodysuit under her suit jacket, would look more professional and be easier on the eye, i.e. less distracting.

Grace grudgingly took my advice and reported back the next week that a Human Resources Director who said he had only twenty minutes to see her had spent two hours talking over his staff problems, and had signed her up for a pilot course then and there. Grace finally realised that she was colourful enough, and made a better impression when she used elegant and subtle colours from her Autumn palette as a backdrop for her wonderful personality.

Frankie's Story

Some of the most rewarding work that we do are makeovers on women who win magazine competitions. Often these are women who have shut themselves off from the world and develop *friends* from the TV or the agony aunts of their favourite magazines. Unlike many regular competition entrants, there are always the special ones for whom this was their first try. They had never won anything in their lives but now they have won the chance of a new image.

Frankie told us that she only wore black because, being a large size, she didn't want to call any attention to herself, and she thought black made her look slimmer. Like many, Frankie had become so despondent about her size she had convinced herself that she was a failure in the looks department and beyond hope. Fortunately, Frankie's sisters and friends felt differently and encouraged her to enter the competition.

We looked at Frankie's naturally blonde hair, peachy skin and clear blue eyes and pronounced that black, in future, could only be worn for funerals. Women with such light, delicate colouring only look older, tired and more beleaguered in black. And, because it is such an over-powering colour, if your own colouring is light everyone else's eye contact will be drawn from your face down to your body – just where you might not want the focus.

As a Light Spring type, Frankie has a range of beautiful colours from clear reds and warm pinks to true blue and violet. But having spent years hiding in black, and just coming out of a bout of minor depression, Frankie couldn't carry off bold colours quite yet. Bold colours require a confident personality, and a readiness to deal with people who will auto-matically be drawn to you. We opted instead for wonderful camels, cream and soft yellows, which were delicate yet colourful, to bring all the attention back to Frankie's beautiful face. And when worn with the right make-up, you were unaware of her size or what she was wearing. All you noticed was her.

Frankie couldn't quite believe the transformation herself. The photo session proved rather difficult as she started to cry every time she saw herself in the mirror, whispering, 'I *can* be pretty'! The last time she said, it, I replied, 'No. You are beautiful when you compliment yourself with these colours.' In future, Frankie agreed to wear black only in her skirts and trousers, and from that day on to bring more colour towards her face and, therefore, into her life.

The Myth about Black

Confession time. What percentage of your wardrobe is black? 50 per cent? 80 per cent? 100 per cent? Like Frankie, I have met too many women whose wardrobes are mainly composed of black, on the absurd assumption that it makes them look slimmer. On the wrong person and when worn in the wrong way, black is a killer which can make you look older, ill, and done in by life. So why do we wear it in such abundance?

The fashion pundits, designers and retailers love black. Indeed, a cheap black anything – dress, skirt, blouse, etc. – looks more expensive than the same garment in a lighter colour. Black is also considered more

ABOVE Larger women often use black to hide their bodies. If black 'wears'you (ie it is too strong for your natural colouring), the focus will be on your body not your face.

ABOVE RIGHT If black does overpower you, be sure to show enough skin at the neck and to wear more make-up to balance with the strength of the colour.

RIGHT The right colours make you look healthy. We notice you first – the great clothes come second.

serviceable as it hides the dirt quite well unless you are a teacher around chalk and a blackboard all day long. But perhaps the best defence of black is that it isn't memorable. Hence, the long-term investment value of a *little black dress* is advised as a wardrobe staple by most fashion editors. You can wear it for years, make it look different with accessories, and no-one's any the wiser.

What about black making you look slimmer? Surely a pair of black trousers are more slimming than the same ones in beige? Indeed, medium to darker shades recede and can make us appear smaller than when we wear lighter colours. So, dark colours are effective when chosen for your skirts or trousers if the lower regions are your biggest problem.

But those black numbers bomb when you wear them on the top half of your body – in your blouses, jackets and sweaters, or all over in a dress – when you don't have the natural colouring to balance with the power of black. For women without striking natural colouring, black requires a lot of work, i.e. make-up, to carry it off. Think about putting on a black T-shirt. How do you look in it in natural daylight without any make-up? If *death warmed up* springs to mind, you are wise to restrict black to your bottom half or to help it along with a colourful scarf or cardigan/jacket.

The only women who can wear black near their face are the Color Me Beautiful seasonal types, Deep Autumns, all Winters and Clear Springs. Their hair type should be dark brown, deep auburn, black or salt 'n pepper. Their skintone should be porcelain, ivory, beige, olive, bronze or deep brown. And their eye colour should be dark brown, clear blue or green or deep hazel.

Discover Your Colours

If you haven't yet discovered which colours bring out your natural best, then it's time you did. The right colours not only make you look wonderful, but they provide the basis of building a working wardrobe. It is both wasteful and frustrating to have a wardrobe that doesn't make any sense, where there are items that can only be worn with one other thing or accessories that have their limitations because of colour. So it is smart for your image as well as your bank account to learn what colours suit you.

A good way to learn what suits you is to turn to your own wardrobe. What items do you love because of the colour? What is it about the colour that you like? Is it soft or is it bright? Does it have a cool, blue undertone to it or would you describe it as a warm colour with yellow undertones? Do you think you glow in strong shades, lighter tones or medium-depth colours? It is the combination of these factors in relation to your own natural colouring – your skintone, eye and hair colour – that determines the right palette of colours for you.

Color Me Beautiful use the seasons of the year to describe women. Initially with only four palettes, like the seasons, we called women Spring types, Summer types, Autumn types and Winter types. After working with many different nationalities, however, we fine-tuned the system to be more accurate and helpful to the many different colouring types. With the publication of my book, *The Complete Style Guide*, we expanded the four seasons into twelve, and there are now three versions for each season.

Confused about your own colouring? Seek an expert's advice. When you discover your best colours, shopping becomes easy.

An easy way to start to assess your own colours is to take one colour, like a green, and see which version is best for you. Compare a pale moss green, a lime green, a blue green and a teal blue. Without any make-up on, hold up a version of these colours (in T-shirts, towels, blouses), and see

1 pale moss green
2 lime green
3 blue green
4 teal blue

which is most flattering. Which one makes your skin look smoothest? Which one makes you look washed out? Which is begging for some make-up?

The right colours are immediate winners, and you know this the minute you wear them. But we can also be 'colour blind' to many shades that are potentially terrific, simply because we've never tried or worn them before. So forget what your mum has told you or what looks great on your best friend. It is probable that neither of them has the same natural colouring as yourself.

Confused? Do you feel you know a few colours that work as well as some that don't, but would like to get better at putting colours together? You have two options to figure out what suits you. First, you can telephone a Color Me Beautiful consultant near you to get information about his or her colour analysis sessions. As it is very difficult to be objective about your appearance and your own colouring, it helps to have a trained eye take you through what to look for and what to avoid. But your other option is to see whether you can determine your dominant colouring characteristics by yourself, from the following pages. Taking it one step at a time, you can discover how to have more fun with colours, and look even better.

To get started, take a look at yourself in the mirror without any make-up, and with a bare neck and chest. How would you describe your colouring? Forget what you looked like when you were younger, and concentrate on your present colouring – unless you colour your hair, in which case consider the colour it is naturally.

Strong and Deep

Women with dark hair and eyes fit into this category and look wonderful in black as well as bold colours like red, purple, emerald green and royal blue.

Light and Delicate

Are you fair in colouring, with almost translucent skin? Blue-eyed blondes and some women with very light grey hair are most suited to light colours.

Warm and Golden

Redheads, women who freckle easily, look wonderful in warm shades. So do the women with mid-brown hair that often has reddish highlights.

Cool and Rosy

These women have pink undertones to their skin and no real golden or red tones in their hair, which can be a beautiful grey to mid- or mousy-brown.

Clear and Bright

These women are noted for the contrast between their dark hair, bright eyes and clear skintone. No sludgy colours for these gals.

Soft and Muted

Women who say that their colouring is 'mousy' really are best described as soft, rich and muted. Indeed, bright colours make them look mousy. They are much more flattered by subdued shades.

On the following pages are examples of the different colour palettes we use. If you can determine which of the six dominant types (above) describes you best, turn to the double page spread showing your two possible wardrobes. You'll see two of our 'seasonal' interpretations for your type. Consider which will be better for you. Perhaps one is stronger, or the pinks are different. Compare and experiment by testing some of the shades yourself. Use your own clothes or towels to assess the different colours.

There are also make-up palettes for each type. Now don't discount what you consider to be your right colouring type just because you have never worn these make-up shades. If you are right about your type, the colours will be fabulous on you. Please note that I have not recommended specific colours for your foundation liquid or creme, as this is too individual; some colours are worn by many different colouring types. So, I have limited the advice here just to colour cosmetics such as lipsticks, blushers and eye-shadows.

See which description of a type fits you best. Don't be swayed by the wardrobe that most nearly resembles your present one, as you may be dressing in colours that really aren't making the most of your natural colouring.

The palette you select will not only look wonderful on you but it will also help you to *organise* your wardrobe. In the range will be some basic neutrals – your investment colours – which will pay endless dividends as they will work with all the other colours in your palette. Also follow the advice on wearing colours according to your body shape in Chapter Two.

STRONG AND DEEP COLOURING

Overall Look:
Projects strength
Hair:
Black, brunette, dark auburn,
salt 'n pepper
Eyes
Brown or hazel
Skintone:
Ivory, rich beige, dark olive, bronze,
black
Famous examples of Deep Women:
Whoopi Goldberg, Isabella Rossellini,
Ruby Wax, Montserrat Caballe
Color Me Beautiful Seasons
Deep Autumn or Deep Winter

The Deep Woman wants to build her wardrobe on strong neutrals such as black, charcoal or navy. But they must always be offset with vivid colours: royal blue, red, bright yellow, turquoise, to name but a few. You are all about contrast, so wear light with dark as opposed to blended monochromatic tones.

Pastels are sickly on you. If you want to wear lighter colours, think *white* with just a hint of colour. We call them icy shades – the lightest pinks, blues, lemons. But these light colours are best reserved for your blouses or sportswear, not for the office in a major item such as a dress.

Your colours are rich, like mahogany, purple, olive and pine green, as well as primary and clear. To make the most of your natural colouring, be bold.

DEEP AUTUMN COLOURS

Add these extra rich colours to your deep palette (shown on the dummy on the facing page) if you are certain that your skintone needs *warm*, not cool, colours near your face and in your make-up.

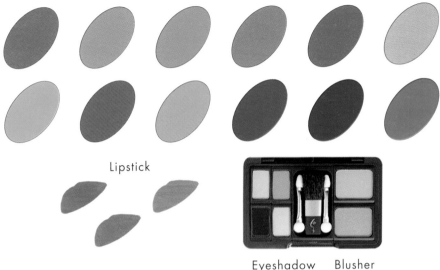

Lipstick

Eyeshadow   Blusher

DEEP WINTER COLOURS

Add these extra rich colours to your deep palette (shown on the dummy on the facing page) if you are sure that *cool*, not warm, colours are better near your face and in your make-up.

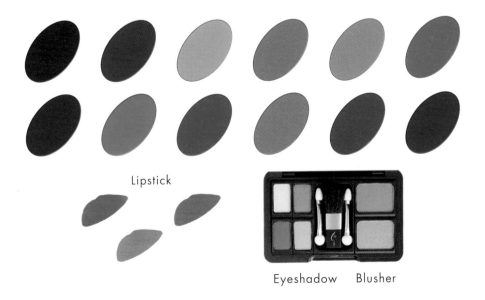

Lipstick

Eyeshadow   Blusher

LIGHT AND DELICATE COLOURING

Overall Look:
Delicate and translucent
Hair:
Blonde or light grey
Eyes:
Blue, blue-grey, aqua, light green
Skintone
Fair – ivory or porcelain, peachy
Famous examples of Light Women:
Tipper Gore, The Princess of Wales,
Peggy Lee, Linda Evans, Gaby Roslin
Color Me Beautiful Seasons:
Light Spring or Light Summer

Your investment colours, i.e. the colours you will be able to wear with anything, range from camel, stone and taupe to soft blue-grey and light navy. Avoid dark, draining colours such as black or charcoal, which only make you look pale. Your white is ivory, but it's better to opt for soft pastels such as apricot, buff, lemon, rose pink or sky blue when you need to offset your strongest colours like navy.

Have fun with bright colours, but be sure not to go too *electric*. Rather than a strong royal blue, try a clear medium blue. A rich purple might overwhelm but if you mix it with blue to make periwinkle you are on to a winner. Blue-greens are particularly nice on light women and are very *friendly* colours.

Your red is best if clear, not too blue or deep. Pinks are fun alternatives when you want a new jacket to brighten up your basic skirts and trousers.

LIGHT SPRING

Add these extra sh... ...y on the
facing page) if you... ...*rm*, not
cool, colours near...

Lipstick

Eyeshadow   Blusher

LIGHT SUMMER COLOURS

Add these lovely colours to your light palette (shown on the dummy on
the facing page) if you are sure that your skintone is better in *cool*, not
warm, colours near your face and in your make-up.

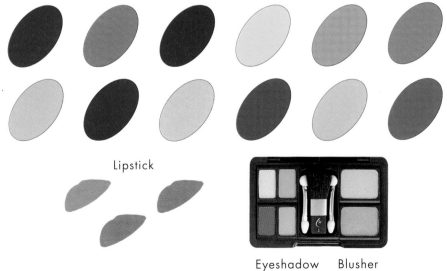

Lipstick

Eyeshadow   Blusher

WARM AND GOLDEN COLOURING

Overall look:
Golden
Hair:
Strawberry blonde, red or auburn
Eyes:
Topaz, hazel, warm green, teal blue
Skintone:
Ivory with freckles, golden brown,
peachy porcelain, yellow beige
Famous examples of Warm Women:
Bette Midler, Emma Thompson,
Jennifer Saunders, The Duchess of
York, Angela Lansbury
Color Me Beautiful Seasons:
Warm Spring or Warm Autumn

Some neutral colours like greys and navies will be losers on you. They don't make the most of your natural colouring. Your best natural bets are golden browns, olives, camels and rusts which are far more flattering to your colouring, and will go with the rest of your colours.

Look for yellow, red or green undertones to your colours. Avoid pure white, and wear cream or buff instead. Choose a brick red rather than burgundy. Your blues are best if 'warmed up' with green – teal blue, for example.

You will look your most exciting if you think of an autumn landscape and put together blended golden tones like moss greens, mustards, terracotta and warm browns. Black is not recommended unless it is kept clear of your face, that is, in your skirts or trousers. But it won't work with all the other wonderful golden tones in your wardrobe. So why buy it?

WARM SPRING COLOURS

Add these extra colours to your basic warm palette (shown on the dummy on the facing page) if your eyes are bright and skin quite fair. These make-up shades will work with everything.

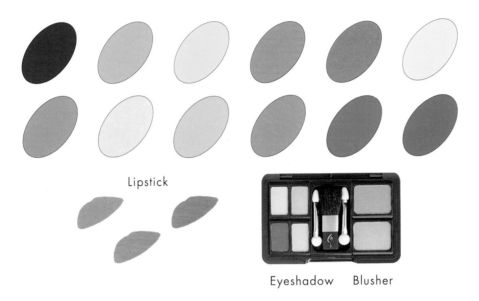

Lipstick

Eyeshadow   Blusher

WARM AUTUMN COLOURS

Add these spicy colours to your basic warm palette (shown on the dummy on the facing page) if your hair is deeper and your skintone richer. These warm, natural make-up tones are your best.

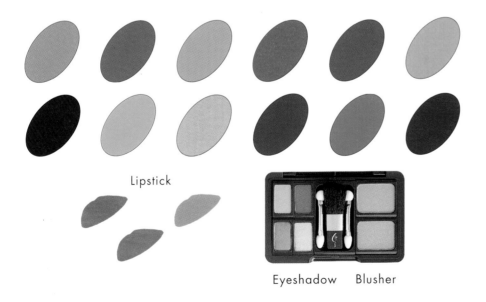

Lipstick

Eyeshadow   Blusher

COOL AND ROSY COLOURING

Overall Look:
Rosy – not light or dark
Hair:
Ash brown or blonde, or grey
Eyes:
Blue or brown (when previous dark hair is now grey)
Skintone:
Pinky, rose-brown, beige, medium olive
Famous examples of Cool Women:
Barbara Bush, Germaine Greer, Anne Diamond, Joan Baez, Joan Plowright
Color Me Beautiful Seasons:
Cool Summer or Cool Winter

Steer clear of most browns, beiges, khaki and cream tones. Your cool colouring looks freshest in blue- or pink-based colours. Great neutral foundations are navy and charcoal, but soften their usually severe impact when they are worn with white, and team them instead with mauve, pastel blue, rose pink or soft fuchsia.

Pastels are wonderful for your blouses, dresses or jackets. However, pastels in a complete outfit aren't strong enough for work, so they are not good choices for a suit. Over an aqua shift dress try a navy swing or 'cardigan' jacket.

Your red has a blue cast to it. The burgundies will work, but test options out to ensure they aren't too ageing.

Very sharp or bright colours can overpower you. Aim rather for richness and subtlety.

COOL SUMMER COLOURS

Add these rich, muted shades to your basic cool palette (shown on the dummy on the facing page) if you know that softer cool shades are better in both your clothes and make-up.

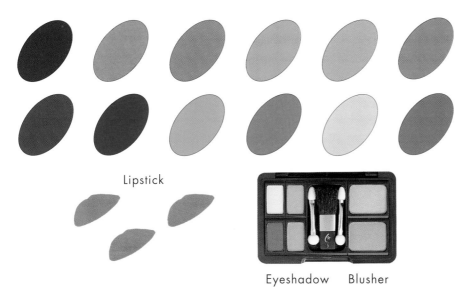

Lipstick

Eyeshadow   Blusher

COOL WINTER COLOURS

Add these stronger shades to your basic cool palette (shown on the dummy on the facing page) if you are sure that you are better in slightly richer cool colours in both your clothes and make-up.

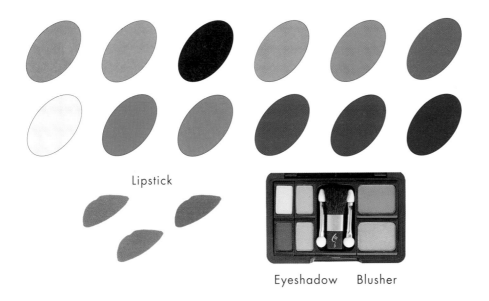

Lipstick

Eyeshadow   Blusher

CLEAR AND BRIGHT COLOURING

Overall Look:
Bright and contrasting
Hair:
Black, brown or rich grey
Eyes:
Steel blue, green, clear hazel or rich brown
Skintone:
Porcelain, ivory, dark ash brown, clear yellow beige
Famous examples of Clear Women:
Roseanne Barr, Oprah Winfrey, Princess Caroline of Monaco, Pauline Collins, Dawn French
Color Me Beautiful Seasons:
Clear Spring or Clear Winter

Use light and dark colours mixed together, or one bold colour on its own. Black, charcoal, royal blue and red will be basics you can mix with many other shades to look your best. Soft monochromatic blends, so elegant on others, will be boring on you regardless of the price or designer label.

Your striking colouring can overwhelm other people, particularly if you limit your colours to strong neutrals such as black and navy. Lighten your impact by using more colour near your face. A bright yellow scarf or jacket will take the 'hard' edge off a black dress. Hot pink makes navy more feminine.

Taupe and pewter can lighten up your summertime work wardrobe but never team with light colours; look to your primaries instead.

CLEAR SPRING COLOURS

Add these colourful extras to your basic clear palette (shown on the dummy on the facing page) if you know you are better in warm-tone colours for both your clothes and make-up.

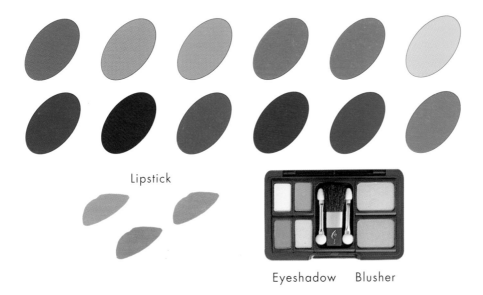

Lipstick

Eyeshadow   Blusher

CLEAR WINTER COLOURS

Add these extra bright colours to your basic clear palette (shown on the dummy on the facing page) if you know you are better in cool-tone shades for both your clothes and make-up.

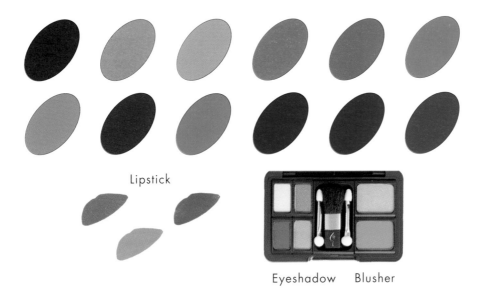

Lipstick

Eyeshadow   Blusher

SOFT AND MUTED COLOURING

Overall Look:
Blended and muted
Hair:
Medium grey, mid or 'mousy' brown,
ash blonde
Eyes:
Blue green, brown, grey blue
Skintone:
Ivory, rose or yellow beige, light olive
Famous examples of Soft Women:
Allison Moyet, Hillary Clinton,
Joanna Lumley, The Princess Royal
Color Me Beautiful Seasons:
Soft Summer or Soft Autumn

These women aren't obviously dark or light but somewhere in between. Bright colours are harsh on them, but that doesn't mean they are limited in looking wonderful.

If you fit this description, your colours need to be rich and blended. Monochromatic dressing – when you use the same hue, but in lighter and darker values – is your best look. For example, you could try ivory, taupe, pewter and bronze mixed together. Something as stark as black and white would overwhelm your soft, subtle colouring.

Your pinks can be either the rose or raspberry tones, if your skin is cool (that is, pinky), or muted salmons if your skin is better complemented by warm colours (that is, more golden or creamy).

SOFT SUMMER COLOURS

Add these rich, elegant extra shades to your basic soft palette (shown on the dummy on the opposite page) if you know that you are better in colours with a cool, not warm, undertone.

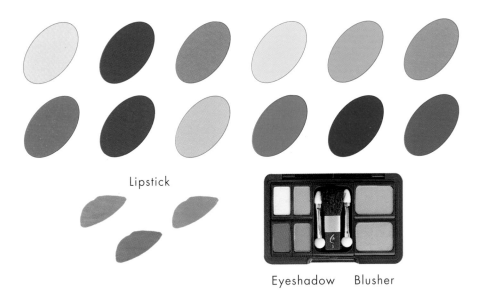

Lipstick

Eyeshadow   Blusher

SOFT AUTUMN COLOURS

Add these rich, somewhat spicy, shades to your basic soft palette (shown on the dummy on the opposite page) if you know that you are better in colours with a warm, not cool, undertone.

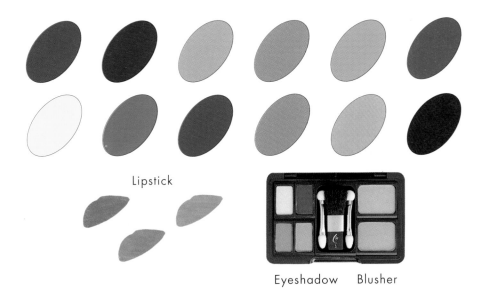

Lipstick

Eyeshadow   Blusher

Colour Illusions

Once you know your best colours it is important to understand how you can use them to flatter your figure. Note the impact of wearing light and dark colours alone or in contrast in the following illustrations. This will help you to discover better ways of putting things together yourself.

All Over Light Outfit When you wear light colours from head to toe, they reflect light and make your figure appear larger than it actually is. Although wearing one colour like this can make you look taller, the overall effect for a women with a full figure is undesirable.

Dark Top/Light Skirt/Dark Legs
Here's a dangerous way to wear colours, particularly if you carry your weight on the hips and thighs. The eye is drawn down from the dark blouse to the skirt which, being light, makes this region look bigger. The effect is exacerbated by further 'chopping up' the body with darker hosiery which shortens the figure and contributes to the widening illusion of the light skirt.

Medium Tone in Top and Skirt

Here's how to wear colours to look your slimmest and your tallest. Choose medium to deep colours from your palette and wear them together in your tops and skirts/trousers. You can brighten the overall effect, while drawing more attention to your face, if you add a colourful scarf.

Light Top/Dark Skirt

Here's how you draw attention upwards, towards your face. This is a possible option if you aren't top heavy, and if you are average to tall in height.

Bright Top/Deep Skirt and Hosiery

Another possible way of looking taller and slimmer, while drawing attention to your face, is to wear a fabulous colour in your top and compliment it with a darker bottom, i.e. skirt and hosiery. When you tone in your hosiery with your skirt and shoes, you get an elongating effect.

Two-Colour Combinations

Neutral with an Accent Colour

Neutral colours provide the greatest versatility for creating many different effects. For drama, wear them alone with one striking accent colour to draw attention where you want it.

Wearing two colours projects a colourful personality!

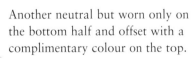

Another neutral but worn only on the bottom half and offset with a complimentary colour on the top.

Colour Tips for Bigger Women

Ask yourself where you want the focus? From Chapter Two in the discussion of your body shape, you will know your best features, the ones offering the most flexibility for style, colour and variety.

If you have a part of your body that you want to distract attention from, then neutralise it with the colours you wear. By a neutralising colour I don't mean a *boring* colour, just one that coordinates with other pieces while not demanding too much attention. Think of a neutralising colour as a nice afterthought: for example, a pewter blouse will *neutralise* a full bust under a rose-coloured jacket better than wearing those colours in reverse. And the impact of such a lovely, unpredictable colour combination is sheer elegance.

On the top half, keep your face the focus by wearing your best colours in blouses, T-shirts, jumpers, jackets and scarves. Try on one of your black jackets on its own in front of the mirror. Now add a terrific colour underneath. Doesn't it look different? So, even if you have a wardrobe full of black, you can transform your image by adding colourful pieces to lift those basics with minimal investment.

If you are top heavy, keep your jackets medium to deep in tone (but only in colours and as deep as your natural colouring can handle), and team with a slightly lighter colour or blend with a complementary patterned skirt. The skirt will be a flirty distraction from your heavier top (and no doubt you have great legs to show off anyway). Don't carry the deep colour in your top right up to your face; relieve its intensity by showing some neck (and, perhaps, accent with a special necklace), or add a personality colour in a scarf or collar. Even though your top half is your problem area, you want to modify its impact while still drawing attention towards your face.

When bottom-heavy, of course, you do the reverse: dark colours in your trousers and skirts and finish the look with toning tights and shoes. But pull out the stops using colour in the top half. The bolder you are there, the less we'll notice those hips and thighs. Using colour like this, along with the style guidelines given in Chapters Two and Three, you can control the focus on your body while expressing your personality.

Colourful Patterns

Selecting patterns can be a challenge for women of every size. But larger women must make sure that not only are the colours complementary, but are also the right scale of print to correspond with your stature.

Have you ever attempted to look *smaller* by wearing bitty prints –

diminutive animals, tiny polka dots or little flowers – only to end up appearing larger than you really are? The dress might fit but the pattern is so out of scale in relation to your height and size that you unwittingly look and feel gormless.

GUIDELINES FOR SELECTING PATTERNS

Petite: 5ft 4in (1.63 metres) and under; size 16+ (12/14+ USA and Canada)

• Small to average size prints   • Blended colours better than bold contrasts   • Limit pattern usage to top half only

Average to Tall: 5ft 5in (1.65 metres) and over; size 16+ (12/14+ USA and Canada)

• Average to large scale prints   • Bold contrasts best on top half only   • Blended patterns effective in matching tops and bottoms • Horizontal lines best if average in size and worn in one long piece; e.g. long jacket, large overblouse, or dress; avoid in skirts alone.

Equally bad is when you try to wear a print that simply isn't *you*. Printed fabrics can be very expressive and make statements about your personality which is what makes patterns so compelling. But the more definite the pattern, the more it should correspond with *you*. Nothing can make you feel more noticeable and uncomfortable than wearing a print that is out of character. I found this with bold stripes. Sure, my colouring can take them, but they simply aren't me. You should be comfortable with your clothes – the colours, styles, details and patterns. If you aren't, those bad choices will be relegated to the back of the wardrobe unworn, and become another wasted investment.

Selecting the best colours in your patterns should be easy for the colour-analysed woman. But how often do our clients come back in a tizzy about whether or not the colours are OK. Once you understand your colouring, you should use the basic principles of your Seasonal Colour Palette as guidance, and not necessarily try to exactly match the swatches that you received in your consultation. They are undoubtedly a good guide to what will be good for you, but they are not the be-all and end-all. It is the overall effect of the colours *together* that determines whether the print will work effectively on you or not.

Experiment with Patterns

If you appreciate that the key thing about your colouring is that you have a soft, muted look, for example, then hold a pattern up near your face and see if the print blends with your muted colouring or overpowers it. This is the starting point. If the pattern seems in harmony with your natural colouring, it has potential.

Now, look at the colours in the pattern itself. What do you have to go with it? Don't immediately reject it if you don't have any of the colours already in your wardrobe. For example, if you are looking at a blouse in an abstract pattern of soft blues and purples and think, 'I don't have any purple or pale blue skirts or trousers', ask yourself what other colours from your wardrobe you could team with it. Anything navy, charcoal, taupe or stone, for example, would work well with a blouse in these shades.

When choosing a print determine whether one colour predominates. If this is the case, then it should link with the rest of your colour palette and be one of your 'best colours'. If a print has a few marginal colours in the background, you can get away with it provided that the dominant colour and overall effect of the print is stunning on you.

Bees to the Honey Pot

What about using colour to attract the opposite sex? Indeed, men and women respond differently to colours. What turns us on can have the opposite effect on the fellas. So, if you are footloose and fancy free, here's some advice on selecting the best colours before a big night out.

Men, unlike women, do not respond well to the muted shades that have been so prevalent in fashion recently. So save the Armani-lookalike for the office, where you can achieve points for looking elegant and professional in those sludgy neutral tones. Oatmeals and beiges are very approachable in business, but leave the dudes cold as ice after work.

Men also instinctively recoil from women in grey. The lighter the shade, the worse the reaction. And, unlike women, especially the Autumn types, who look so wonderful in greens, men actively dislike most shades of green on us.

What men like best are clear, bright colours. They warm up to anything that reminds them of the flesh from the palest peaches and pinks to vivid reds. But when it comes to red, keep it pillar-box and true. Any versions of tomato or rust seem to push them over the edge.

Try blue, if it's you, but keep it true. Navy reminds them of the office.

So change your authoritative navy jacket before dashing from work to meet a man with whom you hope to discuss anything but work!

Now black is a tricky one. It's always portrayed as sensual and romantic, but men need a lot of courage or encouragement from you to respond warmly to you in your black dress. Perhaps it is because it is such a dominant, definite colour. He might be proud to have you on his arm but you won't get him nibbling on your ear until you've dispensed with the black. Also, in black you will have to do all the running as it is the least approachable colour in the spectrum.

CHAPTER 7

EXPRESSING YOUR PERSONALITY

In our style classes, we give women a quiz to determine their *Style Personality*. The six types that we use are, *Natural, Classic, Romantic, Dramatic, Creative* and *Eurochic*. It is very useful to learn your Style Personality to help you get more mileage out of your clothes and accessories. If you are too whimsical and buy without thinking of the personality the clothes or accessories exude, you may end up feeling either boring or ridiculous in them.

So why not see if you are expressing your true personality through your wardrobe, and answer the following questions. Select the best option for each question, even though you might relate to or like two or three of the possibilities. At the end add up how many of each letter you circle to determine your type.

Style Personality Quiz

1. My attitude towards my wardrobe is:

A Comfort, first and foremost.

B I can't stand clutter. Everything must have a purpose.

C My clothes have to be pretty for casual, work or dressy occasions.

D Aside from a few 'around the house' items, all my clothes make a statement.

E The wackier, more diverse and more impossible the better!

F Order and simplicity. Everything is up-to-date and mixes well together.

2. The type of clothes I prefer for work are:

A   Separates that mix and match . . . comfortable yet smart

B   Classically tailored clothes

C   Preferably softer, fluid designs

D   Bold combinations

E   Individual but appropriate

F   Elegantly blended neutral colours

3. The type of clothes I prefer for weekends:

A   Casual, relaxed gear

B   A timeless, good-quality skirt and sweater

C   Pretty blouses and tops; nice shoes

D   Something 'wow'!

E   Ethnic, avant-garde, unpredictable styles

F   Simple but chic

4. My favourite hairstyle is:

A   Casual or windblown

B   Controlled and neat but not severe

C   A soft, layered style; never short

D   Something modern; it changes regularly

E   Spikey, loose curls; uses scarves and clips a lot

F   Current, but timeless, in tip-top condition

5. My favourite fabrics are:

A   Viyella, denim, knits, texture

B   Natural fabrics: 100% wool, cotton, silk

C   Jersey, lace, silk

D   Rich fabrics: velvet, brocade, suede

E   Metallics, leather, contrasting textures

F   Best quality I can find: wool crepe, cashmere, linen

6.   For jewellery I choose:

A   Not much; preferably natural beads and stones

B   Pearls or gold mainly

C   Delicate pieces, also antique jewellery

D   Striking pieces worn for effect, never jumbled together

E   Ethnic earrings and chains. I like to pile 'em on

F   Real jewellery – silver or gold – worn for day and evening

7.   For evening, If I had my choice it would be a:

A   Nice trouser suit

B   Simple black dress – not too short or too long

C   Beautiful dress with lots of detailing

D   Colourful silk jacket or tunic with a plain skirt or pants

E   Kimono or kaftan with all the accessories

F   Smoking jacket and elegant trousers

8.   My favourite shoes are:

A   Trainers or walking shoes

B   Court shoes

C   Higher heels with details

D   Smart boots or whatever's in fashion

E   Funky styles – from ballet slippers to Doc Martins

F   A slight heel in the latest shape

9.   My favourite colours are:

A   Natural dyes, nothing neon

B   Blended colours, not bold contrasts

C   Pastels and brights

D   Rich, bold colours with black or white

E   From neon to hand-painted

F   Neutral colours – charcoal, pewter, ivory or stonewashed shades

10. I would like to develop a style personified by:

A   Roseanne Barr

B   Tipper Gore

C   Elizabeth Taylor

D   Chaka Khan

E   Bette Midler

F   Oprah Winfrey

Answers   If you had mainly **As** you are a *Natural Type*. If you had mainly **Bs** you are a *Classic Type*. If you had mainly **Cs** you are a *Romantic Type*. If you had mainly **Ds** you are a *Dramatic Type*. If you had mainly **Es** you are a *Creative Type*. And if you had mainly **Fs** you are a Eurochic Type.

When you go with your predominant style personality, you get the most mileage out of your wardrobe. Bits will interchange much more easily if, for example, the shoes relate to your clothes for both work and play. Two personality types can blend together in a wardrobe also. For example, if you had a mixture of Natural and Creative, it just means that you like to be comfortable but you also need a bit of flair and individuality to your look. However, some personality types don't mix easily, like the Classic and the Romantic. Wearing a frilly blouse with a tailored suit doesn't quite work. So if you do blend two styles, your weekend clothes and your work clothes, say, try to make them compatible so that you can interchange your clothes more effectively.

If you had a few answers for several different style personalities, your wardrobe is undoubtedly chaotic. You are the woman with a jammed wardrobe who says she never has a thing to wear. You are right: nothing works very well together. So what you have are a bunch of one-off wonders that aren't compatible. It's time to decide who you are and what you like, and to get some sense into your life.

Knowing your dominant Style Personality does not mean that you are stuck to that for life, or that you can't add new things to give your look a fresh twist. The key is to be faithful to the person inside, while making sure that what you choose for your accessories and your clothes compliment your features. For example, many larger women are very feminine and romantic. They love soft fabrics like silk, jersey, and velvet: if it's touchable, it's them. But if very soft fabrics aren't flattering to your figure, the result might be unsuccessful. The answer is not to put you into the opposite of what you like just to suit your size and shape, but to find compromises on style and let your true romantic self be expressed via accessories – a chiffon scarf, delicate dangling earrings, a pretty bracelet, bows on your shoes, an attractive hair clip, etc.

The finishing touches to your image are the signals you send to the world about your personality. Sure, the designs, texture and colour of your clothes will also express who you are, but often when a woman is dressed simply, by choice or convenience, it is her *accessories* that tell others what type of woman she really is.

Think of the signals that you might be sending unwittingly with the bits that you add to your outfits. I remember rushing home on a Saturday after doing a lunchtime presentation, to be greeted by an irritated family long overdue for a walk and mum's company. I quickly changed out of my clothes into some shorts, T-shirt and walking boots. An hour into the walk, when we stumbled upon some friends, it dawned on me that I hadn't taken off my jewellery. I was bedecked in necklace, earrings and bracelets in the middle of the forest in my walking gear, looking pretty ridiculous. Needless to say, the sniggers were quite understandable, and I'm sure they shared a few snide comments about how contrived image consultants are!

There needs to be a relationship between the accessories you wear, the outfit *and* the occasion. But, of course, there are also cultural differences. In France, a woman needs little encouragement to wear a few bracelets at once, while in the Netherlands, if a woman wears more than a modest pair of earrings she feels like a Christmas tree. Indeed, some of my American mates wouldn't see the irony in being caught walking bedecked in gold jewellery – many of them wear the full regalia even when swimming!

When putting accessories together, consider their relationship. Diamanté earrings along with a paisley shawl send mixed signals, with the former being quite dressy and the latter very daytime. But although you want to be careful in teaming things together, you don't want to play things absolutely safe or leave yourself to be packaged like a display in the shops. Even though you might like to wear a matching necklace and earrings for an elegant, classic look, it is fun to see how you can make things look different as well. The more clever and experimental you are with your accessories, the more use you'll get out of them, and you won't feel so guilty when you treat yourself to something new!

THE NATURAL LOOK

You are the woman who often forgets to wear any accessories, even for a party. But that doesn't mean you can't look great with the minimum of accessories. You feel contrived or 'over the top' with too many baubles. But here are some options that will complement your easy, laid-back style.

Earrings
- Plain gold or silver and gold combinations
- Matt, not shiny, metals
- Rough, unpolished stones
- Handcrafted, one-off designs.

Necklaces
- A watch pendant
- Beads on metal, rope or fabric chains
- Simple strand of pearls for evening

Bracelets
- Wooden, hand-carved designs
- Chunky gold chain worn alone or with watch
- Leather straps, plain or with gold motifs

Brooches
- Unfussy, handcrafted designs
- Gold and pearl combination for evening

Scarves
- Plaid, woollen weaves, paisley
- Subtle patterns and colours

Hair Accessories
- They'll drive you crazy. Go without.

ABOVE and LEFT The natural woman looks best when she doesn't even try. Keep the fabrics natural, the fit easy and the colours your best (see Chapter 6).

THE CLASSIC LOOK

A woman who wants an elegant classic look will avoid extremes in her accessories. The key is balance. Earrings should never be too small nor too large, nor should necklaces or bracelets be noisy. You don't want fussy details in your image, so are wise to secure scarves with a brooch rather than leave them to their own devices.

Here are a few ideas for looking classic.

Earrings
- Matt gold, pearl or silver (if hair is grey)
- Diamanté in moderation, e.g. mixed with gold or pearl, not all on its own
- Modest-length dangling earrings (avoid if you have a double chin)
- Gold and stones in fine, controlled settings
- Never more than one earring per ear lobe!

Necklaces
- Within the guidelines for your neck (above)
- One at a time
- Symmetrically arranged stones or one eye-catching piece
- Single or double strand of pearls

Bracelets
- A single bangle, between $\frac{1}{2}$ and 1 in (1–2 cm).
- A gold chain worn with your watch
- An enamel and gold bangle
- Pearl and diamanté combination for evening

Brooches
- Nothing larger than a 50p piece
- Matt gold on its own, or in combination with pearl
- Animal figures that aren't excessively detailed

Scarves
- Paisley, geometric, polka dot, foulard

Hair Accessories
- Simple velvet, leather or grosgrain headbands
- Tortoiseshell clips

THE ROMANTIC LOOK

By nature, you love accessories, and need little encouragement to put on a few every day, even when you are only popping out for a pint of milk or spending the morning gardening!

Very chunky or ethnic accessories look wrong on you, as your delicate and feminine nature requires more intricate details.

Earrings
- If you wear studs, make sure they have detail and aren't plain
- Dangling styles (subject to your neck type, see pages 63–4)
- 'Antique' styles
- Pearl and gold combinations, but in delicate settings
- Glittering stones and diamanté

Necklaces
- No very fine chains, unless worn in a collection
- Lockets with details
- Medium-length string of pearls
- For evening, a chain with a sparkling ornament or pendant that hangs in your cleavage!

Bracelets
- Charm bracelets, but only if your wrist isn't too wide
- Delicate gold and pearl beads worn with your watch
- Velvet and lace bands

Brooches
- Several small pieces worn as a collection
- Cameos
- Diamanté animals
- Delicate hand-crafted gold and silver pieces

Scarves
- Lace, velvet, chiffon, silk
- Soft colours from your palette
- Abstracts, florals, dots or plains
- Lace pocket hankies

Hair Accessories
- Velvet 'scrunchies' rather than hair clips
- Lace treatments
- Chiffon knots

TOP Romantics make the most of their hair and love feminine dresses, especially those that show a bit of leg. BELOW A lacy top, even over jeans, is always romantic.

126

THE DRAMATIC LOOK

These are women who love to be noticed and they know how to use their accessories to great effect. Fashions change, and it is important for them to be up-to-date. They will be combing the magazines and shops to make the right choices on looking current. But here are some general guidelines to help you make the best selections every season.

Earrings
- Bold, striking designs of any material
- Nothing too small unless wearing an earring stud with a dangling design
- Very rough, ethnic designs (unless very *in*) aren't dramatic or versatile enough for you

Necklaces
- Striking, handcrafted silver
- Beads and tassel pendants
- Several strands of gold and/or pearls
- Striking chokers (if your neck allows, see pages 63–4 and 130)

Bracelets
- Several bangles at once
- Large watch on a patent leather strap
- One striking cuff bracelet

Brooches
- Abstract designs
- Conversation pieces – '*Where* did you get that?'
- Any design or material aside from anything too rough or commonplace

Hair Accessories
- Wide velvet bands. Anything more fussy wouldn't be dramatic enough

Scarves
- Large shawls in striking patterns/colours
- Velvet or brocade wraps
- Oblong silk scarves in bold colours
- Plain coloured pocket hankies

THE CREATIVE TYPE

You resist being pegged into any 'type', but know that 'Creative' best describes your style. You make things up as you go along, getting inspiration from films, books, and even your eccentric grannie! The following list will never limit your horizons, but will keep you, I hope, on your wonderfully creative track.

Earrings
- Any number at a time, per ear
- Only one-off, hand-crafted designs or old pieces
- Any material that catches your fancy

Necklaces
- Pile them on or go without as your outfit is bound to be wonderful on its own
- As with the earrings, any material will do

Bracelets
- No traditional, shiny gold numbers, or inconsequential pearl bracelets
- Striking, unique (not necessarily pricey) designs
- Several bangles worn together

Brooches
- Antique designs that aren't too delicate or small
- Bold, ethnic pieces

Scarves
- Any fabric, texture or colour
- A striking pattern worn over plain colours or clashed with other prints

Hair Accessories
- Only ones you make yourself
- Scarves tied in interesting ways

Add necklaces, bangles, boots and a hat to the most simple outfit and *voila!* Or knock'em dead with a wow colour used head to toe like this red one, but never wear sober tights with it.

THE EUROCHIC STYLE

This style personality type is a combination of the Classic, Natural and Dramatic but with an updated elegance that isn't parochial. The look 'travels well' and takes this woman to any event, any time of day. She will follow the guidelines for these three personality types, decide on her favourite two and mix them together in a way that is chic as well as current.

Earrings
- Classy and distinctive

Necklaces
- Go without when wearing special earrings
- Pearls – chokers or multiple strands
- Interesting pendants for casual or dressy

Bracelets
- An elegant watch-bracelet
- Cuff bracelets
- Stone and gold combinations

Brooches
- Never too brassy, sparkling or kooky
- If in doubt go without

Scarves
- Oblong chiffon in sherbet colours for summertime and jewel tones for wintertime
- A large velvet shawl over a simple dress in the evening will be the ultimate in Eurochic

Hair Accessories
- A tortoiseshell clip or velvet hairband

Updated classics that look great anytime, anywhere, become Eurochic.

BELOW The Eurochic woman exudes both confidence and style.

129

Choosing the Best Accessories

Our clients love to learn the tricks of selecting the best shapes, metals/stones and sizes for their accessories. You want them to complement your overall style personality but you also want them to be flattering on you.

Earrings

Earrings are particularly tricky. Why do certain styles work and others not? Rather than always wear the same sort of earrings why not learn what you need to consider when exploring new possibilities. Take out a few pairs from your jewellery box and see how well they work. Sitting in front of the mirror, ask yourself the following questions about each:

- **Is the size in balance with your size?** Very small earrings on a larger woman make you look even larger. If heavy, tall and/or big-boned, opt for more substantially sized earrings.

- **Does the shape flatter your face?** If the earring is wide and your face is full, it will add unwanted width to your cheeks. Better to go for styles that don't protrude, lie flat or hang vertically.

- **Is the colour/metal/stone flattering on you?** No matter how interesting an earring is, if it clashes with your colouring it will only look inexpensive. Test this for yourself. If you have very warm skin-tone, e.g. lots of freckles, hold up a silver earring. Even if it is sterling silver, it will look terrible against your skin and warm hair. The same is true for gold earrings against very beautiful grey hair.

Determine if shiny or matt finishes are best. Maybe you can wear both; but not all women can. Women with 'mousy' brown hair and brown or hazel eyes don't look as elegant in shiny earrings as they do in brushed gold or pearl finishes. In stones, the rougher the better on them rather than very luminous gems – fake or real!

Necklaces

- **Is the length flattering?** Here's where you account for the length and width of your neck and your chin. If you are thick in this area, either go without or only wear long chains. A longer neck will be terrific in shorter, choker styles. If you wear a longer necklace, balance up the space in the neck with a shorter one as well. With long ropes of pearls, double-up and fill in the space.

1 Tiny earrings can look lost on a striking woman.
2 Larger earrings are more in scale with your size.

3 When selecting earrings be sure styles don't add extra width where you don't need it.
4 Longer, dangling earrings can help lengthen a short or full face.

5 Chokers can make your neck look shorter and thicker.
6 Longer necklaces and chains lengthen the upper body.

- **Is the weight of the necklace right for you?**   As with your ear-rings, you need to get the scale or weight of the necklace – the chain and any pendant – in harmony with your own size. A very delicate, fine chain is lost on a strong woman of larger stature, who will look far more interesting in a substantial chain of heavier weight and detail.

- **Is the focus good for your figure?**   It is easy to be swayed by a beautiful pendant, but if you don't assess where it lands on you, it could be disastrous. If full busted, for example, stick to chains, ropes of pearls or a simple pendant that lies flat on top of the bust. Longer styles with bold pendants swing wildly on a full bosom, and only serve to draw attention where you don't need it.

Rings and Bracelets

Rings and bracelets draw attention to your hands. If yours are a good feature, then pile jewellery on within the limits of your own personality. If your fingers are short and podgy, limit the rings to medium-sized ones and only on the ring finger. If you have put on weight, make sure you get your rings re-sized for an easy fit.

Bracelets, like your watch, should never be tight but should slide around easily. If your arms are shorter and wrists thick, limit to one that is neither too delicate (a tiny gold chain, for example) or too thick (like a cuff or several bangles).

Scarves

Scarves can both make or break an outfit. A simple, basic dress can take on a whole new personality with a beautiful scarf. But, likewise, how often have you seen a woman who looks fussy, even ridiculous, because of a scarf that seems to take over her whole outfit.

It will be through some trial and error that you will discover the best scarf possibilities for yourself. Wear a plain outfit to a good department store with a generous selection of scarves, and have a go. If anyone approaches you with dazzling scarf-tying tricks, beware. The most elegant ways to wear scarves are the most simple to achieve. You want to look as though you chose the scarf with some care, put it on and then forgot about it. A scarf that makes you fiddle and fuss all day is a distraction to everyone you are with, and a 'pain in the neck' for you!

CHAPTER 8

GOOD GROOMING

Taking pride in your appearance has a positive effect on your own self-esteem as well as an influence on others. By looking after yourself, you are telling the world that you respect yourself and, therefore, deserve their respect. It doesn't matter that your face, hair or figure aren't perfect. What matters is that you *care* for what you've got. But you don't need to be obsessive with the time and attention you spend on grooming yourself. Most of us only have minutes in the morning and at night, and prefer to be living rather than peering too long into the looking glass. It's only a matter of recognising that your body, like your clothes, requires regular upkeep to look its best.

A wonderful wardrobe can cost serious money while good grooming comes cheap. It is all about making an effort to take care of the condition of your skin, nails, teeth, hair and body that can make your clothes look twice what you really paid for them. Think of women you know who always look polished. Today, good grooming isn't necessarily about having perfectly lacquered fingernails to match your lipstick, or a hairstyle that stays in place regardless of the weather. It's more about looking healthy and finished. So, let's start with the body basics and move through to the finishing strokes to a natural or glamorous make-up.

Body Care

We've all experienced days in which we took too many shortcuts. Perhaps we overslept, had no time to shower, and just jumped into our clothes, pulling a brush through our hair. We left dishevelled and spent the day either trying to hide or trying to compensate for our unfinished state. Leaving the house stale, without proper cleansing, we felt stale all day long. Without basic body cleansing after a night's rest we are also creating staleness and odour in our clothes.

To feel fresh each day requires a morning and evening routine. Even if you bathed before going to bed, you perspire at night and will build up a layer of sweat; this mixes with our natural bacteria and needs eliminating if you want to be odour-free all day. Larger women sometimes perspire more than others, and they particularly require the twice-a-day cleanse.

Twice a Day

A quick shower in the morning is the fastest and easiest way to clean your body. A bath is comforting, but you are never fully rinsed unless you finish off with a shower. Always use a deodorant which will keep you smelling nice as well as prevent your clothes from absorbing too much sweat. Antiperspirants are only necessary if you have a real problem with excessive sweat – they dehydrate the sweat glands so that less is actually produced. This isn't a healthy thing to do every day, for it is important that the body releases as much fluid as it needs to. Reserve antiperspirants for the clammiest of weather, or the most nerve-racking of occasions.

Deodorant soaps smell terrific, but can interfere with your body's own natural cleansing mechanisms. Try a mild soap instead. The objective is simply to wash away sweat and natural body bacteria. Don't use very hot water, which might not only cause you to sweat more profusely after the shower, but will also dry out your skin.

In the evening, a lovely soak in the bath can be very therapeutic as well as good for washing away the day's stale sweat. Be sure to rinse off with a hand-held shower hose or, better still, with a quick shower. If you don't have the inclination or time for an evening bath, a quick shower is recommended, especially if you have had a taxing day and know you have a layer of sweat in certain zones.

The twice-daily cleansing routine is particularly important during the monthly period, when it is essential to keep the genitals clean. Special feminine hygiene sprays or pads are clever marketing ploys, but unnecessary if you are cleansing twice daily. Such products can actually upset the delicate balance of your own system and cause irritations or allergies. Whether you choose to use such products or not, if you notice an odour in the vaginal area it is probably a mild infection which needs medical attention.

BODY-BRUSHING

A great way to increase circulation in your skin is to body-brush. Using a dry natural loofah or a special natural bristle body brush, you brush your skin as firmly as you can stand in circular movements towards the heart. Work your way up your arms and legs, and enlist the help of your partner for hard-to-get-at areas such as the shoulders, backs of the arms and legs, etc.

The benefits of body-brushing are many. Some experts insist that by doing this twice weekly you can shift excess fluid that builds up and causes cellulite. By increasing the circulation in the area, and keeping the pores open there is a better chance that fluids or toxins can be eliminated.

Body-brushing also:

- Evens out the skin and helps prevent the formation of dry patches (especially in the wintertime).

- Prevents 'goose-pimples', which can harden and be rough to touch.

- Helps body moisturisers to be absorbed more efficiently, thus making them more effective.

Skin Care

Make-up should not be used to hide your skin; it should be used to enhance your natural beauty. It follows that the 'canvas' you are going to enhance – your skin – should be the healthiest it can be.

Until fairly recently, many women limited the care of their skin to soap and water. But such simple measures do little to offset the myriad stresses the skins of modern women are forced to face: emotional stresses and strains, unwise foods, as well as environmental pollutants, all of which, bombard and affect our faces daily. However, advances in preventative and restorative skin care mean that we *can* now keep our skins smooth, healthy and even younger-looking.

Determining Your Skin Type

This isn't as complicated as the beauticians would like us to believe. Sometimes your skin can appear drier or oilier than it really is, depending on the products you've been using and how vigorously you've been cleansing. How does your skin look and feel? How would you like it to feel? What would you change about it?

Do the questionnaire opposite to figure out your skin type, then I'll guide you to select the right products to use in a simple three-minute, twice-daily routine.

Step 1: Cleansing

While make-up actually protects your skin from the environment – blocking the damaging and ageing rays of the sun, 'catching' pollutants, etc. – it is still vitally important to remove it thoroughly at night. Soaps made for washing dirt and perspiration off your body are *not* what you want for your face.

Special facial cleansers have been developed specifically to remove make-up and dirt, while conditioning the skin and maintaining its proper 'acid mantle' or pH balance. Choosing a cleanser is a matter both of selecting the right one for your skin type, and personal preference for the formula.

Dry Skin   Choose a cream or creamy-lotion cleanser labelled for your skin type, in a formula that can be rinsed or tissued off. Dry skin cleansers are rich in emollients and oils lacking in your skin, so they leave it clean, but soft. Even if you have wiped off the cleansers with moistened cotton wool, splash your face fifteen times with lukewarm water (over a basin) to help hydrate your skin. Many experts now agree that a daily dosing of warm water can rejuvenate the skin. It's a bit of a bother, but well worth the results.

Normal or Combination Skin   You can choose either a milky lotion or a lathering cleanser. Sometimes a label will read 'For all skin types', but they are always water-soluble, rinse-off cleansers. If right for your skin, it will feel clean and fresh, never tight, after cleansing. If your skin does feel tight, you might try one for dry skin.

Oily Skin   You like the foaming, rinse-off cleanser because it gives you that 'soap and water' feeling of being clean. Don't scrub too hard, let the cleanser do the work instead. Use gentle circular motions to lift all excess dirt and oils. Repeat a second time if necessary.

All Skin Types: Cleansing the Eye Area   The tissue of the eye area is the most vulnerable and requires a special cleanser that is not too rich or too drying. Choose one that is 'Safe for sensitive skin'. Use gentle

FIND YOUR SKIN TYPE

1. After cleansing, my skin's surface feels:

_____ **D**   Very tight and dry

_____ **N**   Slightly tight, but smooth

_____ **O**   Not tight at all; comfortable

2. After cleansing, my skin feels like it needs:

_____ **D**   A rich moisture cream as soon as possible!

_____ **O**   A light moisture lotion

_____ **N**   Nothing; feels fine

3. I suffer blemishes:

_____ **D**   Seldom

_____ **N**   Occasionally

_____ **O**   Often

4. Oil seeps through my makeup:

_____ **D**   Seldom or never

_____ **N**   Late in the day; in nose/forehead/chin areas only

_____ **O**   Within an hour; usually all over

5. My skin looks:

_____ **D**   Dry and flaky; parched and poreless

_____ **N**   Basically smooth and even; small pores

_____ **O**   Rough and coarse; large pores, some blackheads.

Now tally your ticks under **D**(Dry), **N**(Normal), or **O**(Oily) to determine your skin type. If you have three ticks for one skin type and two for another, you will need to adjust your products to the oily side in summertime and to the drier side in the winter.

strokes with cotton wool pad soaked in the cleanser. Be sure all traces of eye make-up are removed.

Step 2: Exfoliate

After cleansing, once a week (twice if your skin is particularly oily), you should use a mask or scrub to deep cleanse and condition your skin. The exfoliation process removes any build-up on the skin's surface, dead skin or blackheads, etc. Choose a mask for your skin type if you have dry skin or 'For any skin type' if normal or oily skin. Follow the instructions carefully about the amount of time required. .

Step 3: Tone

If there is one step women skip, it's this one. Not using a toner is like washing your clothes without putting them in the rinse cycle! Toners remove the last traces of cleanser as well as the deposits from the water (e.g. chlorine), and restore the skin to its natural pH level. Choose one labelled for your skin type, while avoiding any with alcohol, even if you have oily skin.

Step 4: Renew

There is a whole new generation of products available now under the umbrella of Alpha Hydroxy Acids (AHAs), often labelled as 'See visible results', 'Reverses time', 'Younger-looking skin', etc. These products all contain, in varying percentages, one or more acids naturally derived from sugar cane, olives, milk, fruit, or wine, and have been used since the days of Cleopatra to keep skin smooth, soft and even-toned.

What the AHAs do is to 'unglue' or 'melt away' the uppermost dead cells from the horny layer of skin, leaving fresher, newer-looking skin behind. The benefits of using a 'renew' cream are reduced surface wrinkles, a fading of skin discolorations or 'age-spots', and baby-soft skin. AHAs also help to *balance* the skin, so that drier skin benefits more from moisturisers, and oilier skin has fewer breakouts.

Safe and very effective in lower percentages of AHAs (especially when combined with aloe vera), these products can truly give you lovelier skin.

Step 5: Protect

This is the moisturising step, and every skin type needs it. A good moisturiser will not only prevent moisture loss, it will help draw additional moisture to your skin and protect you against damaging effects of the sun (minimum sun protection factor 8). Most moisturisers today add in extra sunfilters (SPFs) to help protect the skin year round.

Dry Skin   Choose a cream or lotion containing a rich blend of natural oils, humectants (moisture attracting), and soothing ingredients, labelled for your skin type. Try it on your neck or the back of your hand. Leave it for 5 minutes. If your skin feels soft and moist (not greasy), this is for you. If you are sensitive to creams, ask for a sample to try for a couple of days to be sure you have no reactions.

Normal/Combination Skin   Look for lotions which list water, aloe and other lightweight ingredients first, and oils later. You need a balance of moisture (water) and oil, as too much oil will leave the skin feeling greasy.

Oily Skin   Even though your skin produces an excess of oil, it does not produce an excess of moisture. Most women with oily skin are prone to *over*-cleanse, which strips needed water *from* the skin. Your moisturiser should be 'oil-free'.

All Skin Types   All women benefit from a good eye cream, since there are no oil glands in the delicate tissue around the eyes. Less is always best, however. Apply using a delicate touch around the orbital bone and over the lid being careful not to go too close to the lashes (which will drag the cream into your eye). Best to use before going to bed. Eye gels as opposed to eye creams are better for wearing during the day; they are absorbed more efficiently and prevent your eyeshadows from going greasy.

Now, all that takes is three minutes twice a day (with an extra five minutes once or twice a week to exfoliate). If you stick to this routine, you may find you never need to have an expensive facial again, unless you want one simply for the treat of it!

Make-up Made Simple

'How did you do that?' is the familiar refrain when we do our makeovers. I never tire of hearing the gasps of delight from audiences when we take a terrific woman and make even more of her natural assets. But there's very little magic about what we do, only some foolproof techniques that you can learn for yourself.

Without make-up, striking features often go unnoticed.

Start with the Right Tools

As any good cook knows, the right equipment can make all the difference in a dish finishing up a success, as opposed to merely all right. But acquiring the right tools of the trade to do a proper make-up is where women often cheat, or make do with the silly utensils that come 'free' with kits.

The Mirror   It should be big enough to see your entire face at one time and, if necessary, have a magnifying area or side to use when applying eye make-up.

Sponges   You'll need a good-quality one to apply your foundation. Keep them to about $\frac{1}{4}$ in (5 mm) thickness, and try different shapes to help you get into crevices (like around the nose). Sponges can also work like erasers when you make a mistake. Clean them in shampoo after every use.

Puff   Foundation is best set with loose powder, and this is best applied with a soft, velour puff. Err on the small rather than large side to help target application.

Tweezers   The sharpest, finest points allow you to get the hairs you aim for rather than a whole clump in the vicinity. Buy from good beauty-supply shops rather than the local chemists.

Brushes   Those that come with your compacts of shadows and blushes are for emergencies only. For achieving professional results, get yourself the following brushes in the best quality you can afford. Natural hairs make application and blending easiest. Wash at least every week in warm water and shampoo, rinsing, shaking off excess water, and shaping. Never leave brushes to soak in water as the hairs and handles will loosen. Brushes can last for years if cared for properly.

- *Blush Brush*   Look for one that is neither too stiff (those leave streaks) nor too soft (the powder will fly everywhere). Dense, rounded-tip brushes pick up just the right amount of colour, deposit it evenly, and blend easily.

- *Eye Blender Brush*   This is the largest brush you will use on the eyes and is sometimes referred to as a 'spatula' brush. Look for one that is firm, dense and flat, yet feels soft on the skin. You will use this for applying highlighter and general blending.

- *Eye Contour Brush*   This is a medium-head, slightly softer brush used for applying medium and deeper tone shadows. It is sometimes called an 'angle' brush if the tip is cut on an angle rather than rounded.

Right and Wrong Make-up Colours
What a difference the right colours can make. Here we show the same techniques using different colours. The wrong make-up colours (LEFT) can make you look overly made-up, while the right ones (RIGHT) make us notice you rather than the make-up.

- *Eye/Lip Liner Brush*   This is the smallest, stiffest brush and you'll need at least two. It is perfect for applying shadow as a liner, powdered brow colour and/or lipstick.

- *Powder Brush*   A short-handled one with a soft, dense, rounded head is ideal for polishing/dusting off excess powder and giving a final blended look.

- *Eyelash Curler*   These should not be dismissed as old-fashioned, as they are vital in helping to open up the eye and make the most of your lashes. Hunt for ones with rubber pads and use gently on the lashes.

Step 1: Foundation

Many women skip this step because they never like the 'feel' of foundation, or think that it looks like a mask. However, foundation helps to even-out skintone, protects the skin from environmental pollutants, and provides the perfect background on which to apply lasting, natural-looking make-up. Foundations today are light on the skin and should be undetectable when chosen and applied properly. Concealer will be used after foundation to minimise its use to only those areas remaining dark or discoloured.

How to Choose a Formula   As with your moisturiser, be guided by your skin type. For very dry skin, creams or creamy liquids are best. For oily skin, water-based, powder-based or oil-free are best. Normal

Choosing the Right Foundation
Dot possible shades along the jaw line. The colour that seems to disappear is nearest to your natural skintone and is your best choice.

skins can use any kind. Microfine powder foundations provide the sheerest coverage; creams the most. Feel them, then try them on to see the amount of coverage you want.

How to Choose a Shade The ideal shade should blend in beautifully with your *natural* skintone and create a neutral background on which to apply your make-up. In the summer when skintone naturally deepens (despite all precautions), you may need to use a shade or two deeper.

If you have problems with ruddiness in your cheeks which fights with your blushers and anything else you put on your face, use a mint-toned colour adjuster on these areas *before* your foundation. Very sallow skin benefits from a lavender colour adjuster before foundation.

How to Apply Get out your sponge. If you want a light finish, slightly dampen the sponge. For more coverage, keep the sponge dry.

Skintone is most uneven in the centre diamond of your face. Begin by applying five dots with a sponge in this centre diamond and blend outwards finally to the hair and jawline. Avoid under the eye area.

Step 2: Concealer

I can go without foundation but I never go without my concealer. Concealer helps to disguise discolorations anywhere on the face, but most noticeably the dark under-circles that are hereditary in some women, acquired in others from ageing, stress, poor nutrition and/or sleeping habits.

How to Choose a Formula Concealers come in lipstick-type tubes or in creamier formulations with a wand applicator. The former type is normally oil-based, and good on normal to dry skin, but the cream formulations are gentler on the skin and easier to apply. Concealer is merely concentrated foundation with some being quite light and others quite opaque.

How to Choose a Shade Try one or two shades lighter than your normal skintone. Stick with natural skin shades, avoiding those that are too pink or too pale. Usually the darker the circles, the more 'purple'-toned they appear. To counteract the purple, choose a more yellow-toned concealer. For 'greener'-toned circles, choose a less yellow, rosier colour.

How to Apply Target your application, resisting the urge to apply to the entire under-eye area. Apply to the darkest area *only* by dabbing the concealer wand in little dots and smoothing in with your ring-finger after you allow the concealer to set or 'warm' to the skin for fifteen to twenty seconds.

Press whatever remaining foundation you have on your sponge under each eye where you applied concealer. Remember if your circles are very dark you may want another application of concealer.

Concealer is also good on age spots and burst capillaries. Use on blemishes only if you are certain of the formulation's medicinal properties (packaging should specify). Only use on spots that haven't been disturbed (i.e. popped or opened with exfoliation).

Step 3: Eye Shadow Base

Ever wonder why the shade of shadow you bought doesn't look quite the same on, or worse, doesn't *stay* on? Look at all the natural colouring in your eyelids. Applying eyeshadow straight on is like putting pale pink paint on a beige wall, and wondering why it comes out a muddy mauve.

An eye shadow base acts as a primer to even out skintone, so colours look and stay true, and as a 'magnet' to keep shadow in place all day.

How to Choose a Formula   While all are water-based, they come in different forms, from an easy-to-use mascara-like tube (with a soft-tip applicator), to squeeze tubes and pots. Choose whichever is easiest to apply.

How to Choose a Shade   This is usually done for you as they only come in a light, natural shade.

How to Apply   Put a small amount on the tip of the ring-finger, dot over lids and blend quickly from the lashline to the brow. Allow the base to 'set' for a few seconds.

Step 4: Loose Powder

Without using powder to set your foundation, your blusher will 'grab' on to your cheeks and look quite startling. When applied over liquid foundation, loose powder gives a soft-focus finish. Powders today are not heavy and dry. They are sheer and undetectable, and often contain beneficial moisturising ingredients and age-defying light reflectors. Most loose powders are a similar formulation.

How to Choose a Shade   There is no such thing as a totally 'translucent', i.e. colourless powder. Choose a shade that matches closely your foundation/natural skintone. A powder that's too light is ageing, while one too dark makes the skin look muddy.

How to Apply   Lightly cover one side of your velour puff with powder then press gently, yet firmly over the entire face, concentrating on the centre diamond, especially if you tend to have a shinier nose during the day. Use your powder brush to dust off excess.

Step 5: Eye Pencil

Use eye pencils to add depth to the eyes and to create a bit of drama.

How to Choose a Formula   Liquid eyeliner is used only for effect and is difficult to control for all but the experts. Kohl pencils are best for adding definition as well as giving you lots of possibilities for creating different colours and effects. Best to apply over your base *before* shadows.

For best effect, always use a sharpened pencil. If the texture is not soft enough, 'warm-up' by rubbing on the back of your hand.

How to Choose a Shade   For a natural look, choose a shade the depth of your hair colour and which blends with your eye colour, e.g. chocolate brown for brunettes, charcoal or navy for ash blonde or grey tones, copper for redheads, soft brown/taupe for blondes. For more ideas on colour, see recommended shades under the colour palettes in Chapter Six.

How to Apply   Picture an imaginary line drawn from the nostril to the outside tip of your brow. This is the *outside* parameter of where you will apply your eye make-up.

Holding the eyelid taut, begin the line at the outside corner and draw it three-quarters of the way to, but not over the crest of, your lashline, as this goes over the centre of your eyeball. Draw as narrow a line as possible (easiest if you look down into the mirror while keeping your head erect).

Blend the line softly with a cotton swab or your finger tip over the crest towards your nose.

For even more drama, add a line to the lower eye, starting from the outside edge working a quarter of the way in. This forms a V at the outside corner of the eyes.

Never forget that encircling the eyes completely with an eye pencil 'closes' them in, and makes them appear smaller. Accentuating the outside corner with the above described V opens up the eye area and makes all eyes appear more dramatic.

Step 6: Highlighter

The palest shades like ivory, peach, lemon and pink are used to lighten areas of the eye that you want to bring forward, e.g. under the brow (orbital bone); the centre of the eyelid; and the inside corner of the eye.

How to Choose a Formula   As with blusher, powder highlighters are the most natural and easiest to apply, especially with a good brush. They are also available in creams in tubes, pots and lipstick-type applicators, but they are more difficult to use if you want a natural look. Stay away from highly pearlised formulas as they look artificial and are ageing on most eyes over 30.

How to Choose a Shade   The highlighter is used to bring parts of the eye 'out' or 'forward'. Hence, you use the lightest colours from your palette, e.g. champagne, melon, pale pink, apricot, etc. (see the colour palettes in Chapter Six and the Colour Appendix for more details).

How to Apply   Use the eyeshadow blender brush, and dust over the entire eye area all the way from the lashline to the browline. This softens your pencil line and acts as a neutralising backdrop for other shades. Only use matt colours.

Step 7: Contour colour

Contouring gives shape and depth to the eyes. This is what can transform the most slapdash application into real drama.

How to Choose a Formula   As with your highlighter, powder shadows are most natural and easiest to apply with a good brush. Cream shadows, or those in tubes or sticks, are more difficult to apply, and will rarely look natural.

How to Choose a Colour   In your cosmetic colour palette, there will be medium-depth neutral shades to use for contouring such as cocoa, taupe, pewter or soft grey. Save the colour-colours like your greens, blues and violets for strategic effects, e.g. a dash in the centre of the lid, or to add mystery over your eye pencil.

How to Apply   Look into the mirror and see where your eye is most prominent. For most of us, it is the fleshy area over the orbital bone that can hang down on to the lid. This is the area to contour.

Apply the contour colour with your eyes open, not holding the skin taut. Using the eye contour brush, stroke over the shadow, tapping off

Eyes
Bring out the beauty of your eyes:
• lighter shadow on the inner corner helps to widen the eyes
• soft khol pencils can be used on both the top and lower lids to make the lashes appear thicker. Prevent your eyeliner smudging by 'setting' with eyeshadow
• soft browns, greys, navies and greens are best for softening the orbital bone
• a lighter shadow just under the brow and the lid will brighten all eyes.

any excess on the back of your hand. Beginning just inside your outside boundary (described in Step 5), glide the brush across the most prominent area only.

Now go back and soften all the edges with a brush or your fingertip so the shadow has no top or bottom demarcation lines.

Connect the contouring shadow to the lashline by means of a 'triangle' which is naturally formed by the orbital bone and lashline. The farther away your bone is from your lashline, the bigger your triangle. Again, softly blend all edges.

Soft neutral shades help to give the eye even more shape than it might have. Hence, if you have a large orbital bone which looks puffy if left natural, a soft blending of a midtone neutral over this area will subdue its effect and give the eye depth.

Step 8: Definition Tricks

It is step-back time to see if any area of the eye needs more definition. This can mean going over your eye pencil with a fine touch of shadow (which will deepen the colour as well as prevent smudging), or adding a richer colour to your triangle. For example, if you chose cocoa as a contour, try an aubergine or rich neutral brown for defining; if you used a soft grey contour, try a navy now for effect. A soft camel or sage can be enhanced by a deep olive.

Step 9: Eyebrow Colour

Leaving the eyebrows unattended is like hanging a picture without a frame. Your browline should be neat and clean, and enhance the shape of your eye. The natural brow look is best and, despite the vagaries of fashion, always looks right on *real people*. Tweeze clean any straggling hairs that make no contribution to the overall effect or that drag the brows downwards to make you look sad.

How to Choose a Formula Cake/powdered brow colour is easiest to apply, although many natural tone eyeshadows can be used for the purpose. Brow or eye pencils can also be used.

How to Choose a Shade Try to get a shade as close to your hair colour as possible. If very blonde or grey, go one or two shades deeper; if very dark, you may want to go one shade or so lighter for a softening effect.

How to Apply Use feather-like strokes along the brow to the outer edge but not beyond the boundaries described in Step 6. Now go back against the hair grain with similar strokes. Finally, brush the brows upwards and outwards with a small comb or brow brush. For really troublesome brows, try a touch of clear hair gel on your brow comb to keep them in place.

Step 10: Mascara

A creamy formulation that lengthens and deepens the eyelashes.

How to Choose a Formula   The mascara you choose depends on two things: your lashes and your lifestyle. The formulas that are available include lash thickening, lengthening, building (a combination of the first two), and waterproof. The best overall choice is a water-resistant, lash-building formula. If your life is active and you need your mascara to hold up to any amount of dips in a pool, then a waterproof mascara might be better. Just be prepared for some effort to get it off eventually.

How to Choose a Shade   Use the strength of your hair colour as a guide. Consider other colours that will enhance and not look bizarre, like navy with grey or blonde hair (rather than light blue), aubergine on brunettes or bronze on redheads.

How to Apply   A slow wiggling motion all the way from the base to the tops of the lashes works best. Concentrate colour on the outer half to 'open' up the eyes. For extra full lashes, repeat the procedure twice in succession without allowing drying in between. Applying with your mouth opens help you to target more successfully!

   Turn the brush vertically to reach the tiny bottom lashes. One coat is enough, especially for the over-30s.

Step 11: Blusher

Blusher should not appear as two dots in the centre of cheeks or as 'apples' or racing stripes across the cheekbones. When you use the right colour, intensity and application, it should lend a healthy natural glow to your skin. It is best to apply blusher after your eyeshadow so that you match the intensity of the colour and effect of your eyes with your blusher.

How to Choose a Formula   Powder blusher gives the most natural look, and is easiest to apply. Blusher also comes in creams, mousses and gels which must be applied with the fingers, and are harder to control.

How to Choose a Shade   Here's where knowing your Seasonal Type

Apply blusher in upward strokes from the cheekbone to the temple.

is essential. For each Color Me Beautiful Season there are guidelines for all your colour cosmetics (see pages 100–110 for suggestion). Keep in mind that your most neutral or natural shades are a good place to start. Once you build up your confidence, you can explore more options. All women need a deeper blusher for evening (just to look healthy!).

Think of your blusher, shadows and lipsticks as collections of colour. They should coordinate with each other – that is, not brown blusher with pink lipstick and blue eyeshadow! See our coordinated make-up colour charts for guidance.

How to Apply   There are a few simple rules.

- *Don't*   Apply too close to the eyes as it will accentuate lines and make your eyes look puffy.

- *Don't*   Apply too close to the nose, or your cheeks will look 'cherubically chubby'.

- *Don't*   Apply too far down the cheeks, or in too large an area, or the face will look heavy and feverish.

- *Do*   Stroke the brush gently across the blusher once or twice, then tap the excess on the back of your hand before applying. Remember, it's easier to build a colour with a second application than to tone down a too-bright or too-strong colour.

- *Do*   Apply along the bottom edge of the cheekbone (not above). Feel the bone with your fingers. Start at the point directly below the outside of your iris, but not below the cleft of the nose (where it joins the face above the lips). Blend out to hairline.

- *Do*   Once applied, blend upward (to top edge of cheekbone) and outward. No definite edges should be visible.

If your face is very round or very narrow and long, you will apply blusher on a slightly different angle.

The goal is to add angles to the round face and softness to the angular face, not to mimic and thus emphasise the roundness or narrowness.

Step 12: Lip Pencil

As we age, our lip line loses definition. And some of us have unbalanced lips – too large, too small or lop-sided. Lip pencils can help to balance

ELONGATING TRICKS FOR FULL FACES

- **Arch the eyebrows**   Work to define the brows from above not below. Clean out stray hairs from under the brow. Enhance your own arch using soft shadows that match or are slightly lighter in colour to your brow.

- **Creative blushers**   Take a natural blush colour (in a brown that compliments your own colouring, e.g. rosy, peachy or cinnamon) and brush from the temples down along the side of the face sweeping softly to under the cheekbone – but not to the jawline. Avoid an obvious 'stripe' of colour; softened edges are best. Now press a lighter or brighter blusher (from your colour palette) right in the apple of the cheek.

- **Double chins**   Keep your chinbone light with translucent powder and 'negate' the others underneath by using a deeper blusher, contouring powder or bronzer. Dust gently, avoiding obvious patches of light and dark by blending.

Dust under your chin with a soft brown blush or bronzing powder to minimise the effect of a double chin.

- **Slim the cheeks**   Use a contouring powder (again, a soft brown blusher or a matt bronzer), from where there should be a hollow under the cheekbone down along the jawbone. Check the sideview in the mirror to ensure you have blended well and avoided an obvious stripe.

    Now lighten the outer eye area and temples with a very light blusher. The effect will be to draw attention to the eyes while the deeper blusher below minimises the cheeks. Use a lighter, brighter blusher on the apple of the cheeks up to the cheekbone.

- **Luscious lips**   Full lips are an asset, but if yours are too ample, outline *inside* your lips and use medium to deeper lipsticks in matt finishes. Avoid glosses.

out lips, whatever shape they are. They are also great for preventing the 'feathering' or 'bleeding' of lipstick.

How to Choose a Formula   These should be creamy, but not soft. As with an eye pencil, you must keep them freshly sharpened for best effect.

How to Choose a Shade   You'll want to coordinate with your lipstick. Either match the shade or choose one shade deeper if you are using the pencil for definition. Lip pencils can also be used to create different colours with your lipsticks. To get started, try a natural shade, the same colour as your lips or the inside of your lip.

How to Apply

1. *For balanced lips*, apply along the lip line.

2. *For small lips*, apply along the outside edge of the lip line.

3. *For large lips*, apply just inside the natural lip line and 'scribble' over the heaviest part of the lip.

4. *For uneven lips* (one lip or one side of same lip small, the other large), use a combination of 1 and 2.

If you use lip base and/or lip pencil (to outline and fill in the lips) before applying lipstick, your lip colour will last for hours.

Step 13: Lipstick

This is every woman's staple beauty product and instant face brightener. Many women have a whole wardrobe of lipsticks, others just one or two favourites.

How to Choose a Formula   Personal preference is what matters as formulas range from ultra-creamy (preferred by women with dry lips), to dry-as-a-bone matt; all come in pearlised and matt shades. The more vivid or blue-red the colour, the more matt the formula and the longer it will last. Older women are advised not to wear pearlised shades (which can be ageing).

How to Choose a Shade   Select one from your palette as part of your collection to coordinate with your wardrobe. Basic, neutral shades are listed for every type in the Colour Appendix on pages 166–70.

How to Apply   Try not to apply directly from the tube (except in emergencies) but use a lip brush. A lip base, applied first, will help the lipstick last longer and help give you a perfect finish.

Stroke the brush back and forth over the lipstick then use short, vertical, up and down strokes to cover the lip area, keeping within the lip pencil.

Once you have filled in the lip surface, use what's left on the brush to smooth on, but not beyond the pencil, blending the two.

There you have your basic, daily make-up routine. It might have taken you a few minutes to read and maybe twenty minutes or so to teach yourself the steps. But all it should take *to do* is ten minutes or less. On the days that you don't have even ten minutes, do the basics – a little concealer (if necessary), a quick dusting of powder-foundation, a dash of blush, mascara and lipstick, and you'll be ready to face the world.

Nail Care

Any expressive woman who makes extensive use of gestures when speaking should appreciate that her hands are integral to her image. If a woman is beautifully made-up yet has miserable, unmanicured nails, she is sending mixed signals.

For busy women with demanding schedules, long or artificial talons are unrealistic, considering the necessary upkeep involved in maintaining their condition. Keeping your nails short to medium in length, and well-maintained by regular use of a cuticle and hand cream, is all that is needed. The shape of the nails should mimic the fingertip shape. Always soak your nails first before removing cuticles. If they tend to get rough and dry massage them with some olive oil and leave to be absorbed overnight. The best colours for varnishes are neutrals that can go with everything (e.g. a clear or pale tone), or a colour to coordinate with your favourite lipstick.

For women keen to keep all the attention on themselves, longer, stronger, more colourful nails will do it every time. Think of a woman with beautifully manicured nails and consider how important they are to her image. They simply *are* her! Thanks to the wonders of modern science, any of us can have gorgeous nails even if we weren't blessed with them naturally. All it takes is some time and money at the local nail clinic, and refusing ever to pull a weed or do the washing-up again! Basic good grooming requires that you don't go out with chipped or broken nails, and you should carry an emery board around in your handbag for emergencies.

For very dry hands, try wearing lashings of Vaseline inside a pair of cotton gloves while you sleep. This takes some getting used to, but the combination of the warmth and the Vaseline produce baby-soft hands.

Hair Care

We all complain about our hair. If only it wasn't the way it is . . . if only it was longer, fuller, curlier, straighter, lighter, darker, shinier, etc. With the products available today, we can all transform our natural manes into just about anything we want. What it takes is an appreciation of our own features first – face shape, hair texture and colouring – and consideration of our lifestyle, i.e. how much time we are prepared to spend attending to our locks. Another key factor is the stylist we choose to do our hair.

Enhancing your Locks
Perms can add welcome volume to lifeless, fine hair but be sure the style is flattering (RIGHT). Full, frizzy, shapeless perms add weight and years to the face (LEFT).

Face Shape

Here are some simple tips for choosing the best options for your hairstyle.

Oval Faces   These have limitless possibilities in terms of style, and will only be restricted by the texture of their hair, and the time they are willing to devote to caring for it.

Round Faces   Avoid perky bubble cuts or curved bobs that will simply repeat the roundness of your face. Try something more angular to frame the roundness of your face. Curly or straight hair can be cut sharply to complement a round face successfully.

Oblong Face   A long face looks sad, tired and older in long straight hair. Get some balance by 'breaking up' your face with a shorter fuller style. If your face and neck are long, go for medium-length hair (to 'break up' the length of your neck) but add some layers around the face, e.g. a soft fringe, wisps at the side, etc.

Square Face   A short and wide face gets buried in long, full styles. It's best to have a cut

Flatter Your Face Shape
Flat hair does nothing for an oblong face which always looks more balanced with shorter, fuller styles.

that doesn't end at your jawline, and that is layered on the sides. You need a lift at the crown so shorter styles layered on top are particularly good.

All face shapes   Remember to consider the effect of a new style from the front, side and back. A style that seems to frame your face perfectly from the front can squash you into your neck from the side. If a double chin or full neck is an issue, a style that lifts the face i.e. short and layered or long hair worn up in a twist or French pleat, will be more becoming than a bob that ends in your danger zone.

Colouring Tips

If considering a new effect with hair colour, it is advisable to seek the help of a colourist who specialises in the latest techniques and uses a product range that has a good formulation for your hair texture.

New colourings don't just add colour. They add shine as well as condition, and can create texture and depth you never thought possible. Never before has home hair colouring been so easy; yes, almost foolproof provided that you follow instructions.

Temporary Colours   The fastest and most simple to use are temporary colours that simply shampoo into the hair. Large colour molecules coat the outside and cuticle layer of the hair only. Colour washes out in one to six shampoos.

Colour Setting Lotions   These combine a temporary colour, which usually washes out after one shampoo, with a strong setting lotion to help with a style you might like to create. Great for the hot party on Saturday night!

Semi-permanent Colours   These can only enrich or darken hair, not make hair lighter. Colour molecules penetrate the cuticle, and coat the outer edge of the cortex (inner layer of hair). They last for up to twelve shampoos.

Longer-lasting Semis   As with the above, these are only for dark hair but last for from twelve to twenty shampoos. The colour eventually fades, so there are no regrowth considerations as with permanent colours. These are stronger, so if you have a perm, leave for a couple of weeks before trying one of these colourings. Good on grey hair if you just want to deepen about 50 per cent of the grey.

Permanent Colour   These will lighten, darken or cover grey. The colour will not wash out or fade too much but has to grow out with your hair. Roots need retouching every six weeks, but be careful not to go over previously treated hair or you get a build-up of uneven colour. Only consider permanent colour if you're dead certain about the colour and desired effect.

Choosing the Right Colour

Use your natural colouring as a guide to the range of possibilities for enhancing your hair colour. Best advice is not to go too far away from your genes – either too light or too dark.

Blondes   Get the undertone right for your skin. If you have warm skintone, golden highlights will be more flattering than ash ones. For neutral/beige skintone, ash highlights will be more elegant.

Mousy Brown Hair   You benefit from highlights or a chestnut colour rinse that isn't too dark. Don't go very deep brown or auburn.

Mid-brown hair   Think twice about highlights. If you go too light you will look older. Adding depth and sheen with a semi-permanent might be a better bet.

Deep-Brown Hair   Avoid 'blackening' your hair. Better to enrich with a deep chestnut or auburn colouring.

Redheads   If your eyes are blue and your skin very pale, golden highlights or a red rinse are a nice possibility. If you have stronger skin and eyes, you can go redder or more auburn, but not blonde.

Grey Hair   Be honest about the grey. If it is a dishwater shade, it will probably look better covered in a shade lighter than your original colour. If it is rich 'salt 'n pepper', or a pearl grey, why not leave it rather than going through the agonies of constantly retouching to hide the roots. Many blondes who go grey should let their highlights grow out, and appreciate that their own new natural grey highlights are just as lovely as those from a bottle.

CHAPTER 9

FIT NOT FAT

I've saved the preaching for last. In every one of my books there is a chapter on fitness, because I am a fitness freak. This is for health as well as image reasons, for I have two daughters, and I want to be around to appreciate them as well as their children. I don't want to be a fragile mum unable to participate in their rough-and-tumble lives. Nor do I want them to worry about me more than is normal due to failing health later in life.

Your state of fitness is as much a health issue as it is a career issue – one that can affect your chances of getting a job and getting promoted. But before you slam the book shut, fearing a lecture on being overweight, read what I mean by 'fit'. Size isn't the problem, rather it's the perceptions others have about your vitality. A fit person has energy, life, bounce and can contribute – no holds barred. The research we did for the *Presenting Yourself* books confirmed that top employers sought candidates that were 'fit and healthy', the fit image coming second in importance in a job interview to wearing a smart outfit and looking the part. So, fitness is as good for your career as it is for your health *and* your self-esteem.

I know, I know. Many women who are larger are as fit, if not fitter, than many smaller women. I'm not referring to these terrific amazons. I am talking about the couch potatoes, whether they are a size 10, 20 or 30. You know who you are. Yes, you are the ones who always opt for the escalator, viewing those who bound up the stairs as nothing short of mad. You fail to monitor your intake of fuel or calories in food with the amount of energy you burn on a daily basis. You blame your lethargy as well as the dimension of your thighs on your genes, the stress in your life, and a variety of other excuses, failing to accept that your fitness is up to you, and you alone.

How Fit Are You?

Consider the following:

- Can you climb two flights of stairs at a steady rate without getting breathless?

- Can you get ready in fifteen minutes in the morning?

- At a nightclub are you able to dance for up to twenty minutes without a break?

- Do you feel sluggish after lunch?

- Do you stretch out on the floor and do a few limbering-up exercises regularly?

- If you sit on the floor, can you get up without holding on to anyone/anything?

- Do you find a walk along a sandy beach a struggle?

- Can you pull yourself out of the swimming pool without using the ladder?

- Do you know how much food you need to eat without putting on weight?

- Do you control your eating from time to time to feel better?

- Do you require a lot of sleep and feel the need to compensate with extra rest at the weekends?

If any of these questions have you thinking 'I really should be able to do that', then maybe it's time to improve your fitness. It will help you worry less about your weight, and make you feel more full of life.

Dieting Is No Panacea

Our weight is not entirely within our control, so stop blaming yourself for being a 'failed dieter'. Recent studies prove that our genes largely predetermine body shape and, to some extent, body fat. Heredity also influences how food is metabolised. Think of your own parents, aunts and uncles. Is your shape reminiscent of Aunt Agatha's? Just because you inherited Agatha's tummy isn't an excuse not to keep fit and toned. You might never have an hourglass figure due to your genetic predisposition, but you *can* have a waist that is neat and toned, which will prove you to be a woman who is in control of her body.

157

A genetic proclivity towards retaining weight can be made worse if you have a history of excessive dieting, because rigorous dieting lowers your basal metabolic rate. Your metabolism is the process by which your body transforms food into energy and then expends the energy. Through dieting you end up needing fewer calories to exist. So when you begin eating normally, or worse, celebrating the weight loss, you pack on the pounds faster than ever. Biochemical changes in the body through cyclical dieting also increase the percentage of calories that are stored as fat.

So it is no surprise that most studies show that for every 100 people who lose weight, about 95 will regain as much as they lose. Successful dieting is defined as reaching your ideal body weight and maintaining it for five years – similar to going through a full remission from cancer. Reflect on your own success with controlled eating regimes. How long were you able to sustain a decent weight loss when focussed on food alone? Weight loss and maintenance is only possible through a combination of sensible eating (*not dieting*) and exercise.

Body Fat Is the Culprit

The ratio of body fat to muscle is the key to vitality and health. Whatever our size, we should know how much of us is made up of a healthy amount of fat, and when that ratio becomes a health hazard. If, in addition to having a high amount of body fat, you hold that fat in the stomach region (rather than in the hips and thighs), you run a greater risk of heart disease and diabetes if you are also overweight. Fat carried in the hips and thighs is supported by the larger, stronger leg muscles, putting less pressure on the internal organs, including the heart.

To calculate your ratio of fat of the waist to the hips and thighs:

Measure your waist 2 in (5 cm) above the navel
Measure the widest place on your hip/thigh
Divide the waist by your hips

A ratio of 0.8 or more means that you are running a greater health risk (men, 1.0 or more).

Your Ideal Weight

Your weight is a starting point in assessing your level of fitness and vitality. You don't need a set of scales at home to haunt you daily, but should check in with your doctor each year to get an objective accounting of your weight. Weight-Watchers have probably done more for women and men seeking a major change in lifestyle through sensible eating and

PERFECT POSTURE

Everyone looks slimmer, taller *and* younger if they move correctly. Years of bad habits – slouching, sitting on bad chairs, sleeping on wrong mattresses, etc. – can cause our frames to become totally 'unaligned'. Some of us can correct bad posture simply by becoming aware of ourselves and moving better. Others need the trained eye and skills of an expert to teach us how to move more effectively.

Some larger women develop bad posture at a young age to 'hide' their bodies. Think back to school, and how some of the taller girls and those whose breasts were more adult than adolescent, 'caved in' with rounded shoulders to make them appear shorter or smaller. As a result, clothes never hang properly, nor can you make the most of your figure. You can literally look sizes smaller if you learn to carry yourself better.

The benefits of good posture are not only aesthetic but also therapeutic. Holding yourself properly and in balance reduces strain on the body – our skeleton and joints – and enables us to live longer without aches and pains.

If your posture is letting and getting you down, consider a consultation with a practitioner of the Alexander Technique, who can reverse years of poor posture within weeks. You will not only look better, but are sure to find yourself enjoying more of life with less strain.

exercise than any other organisation. Their guidelines for weight aren't aesthetically based, but are determined by what is medically sound for us by height. See their height/weight chart on the following page.

If the chart worries you, then perhaps it's time that you had your fuel intake (i.e. the food you eat) and your energy expenditure (i.e. the amount of exercise you take) professionally assessed. If there is a major imbalance – eating the wrong foods and/or just too much food, and not enough exercise – we put on weight and become unfit. And when you are unfit, you are unable to live life to its fullest. The large and unfit also suffer prejudice, in their personal lives and their careers. So, if you are teetering on the brink of an unfit and unhappy state, it's time to take yourself in hand with exercise.

Goal Weight

Find out your ideal weight

In stones and pounds for men and women

Height Without shoes in ft. in	Min Joining weight in st. lb	Women 16–25 Yrs Healthy Range	Women 26–45 Yrs Healthy Range	Women 46 Yrs + Healthy Range	Men 16 Yrs and over Healthy Range	Max. allowed	Height Without shoes in metres
4' 6"	6.11	6.1 - 6.9	6.1 - 6.12	6.1 - 7.2	6.1 - 7.6	8.1	1.37m
4' 7"	6.12	6.2 - 6.12	6.2 - 7.1	6.2 - 7.6	6.2 - 7.10	8.5	1.40m
4' 8"	7.0	6.4 - 7.2	6.4 - 7.5	6.4 - 7.10	6.4 - 8.0	8.9	1.42m
4' 9"	7.4	6.8 - 7.5	6.8 - 7.9	6.8 - 8.0	6.8 - 8.4	8.13	1.45m
4' 10"	7.7	6.11 - 7.9	6.11 - 7.13	6.11 - 8.3	6.11 - 8.8	9.4	1.47m
4' 11"	7.10	7.0 - 7.12	7.0 - 8.3	7.0 - 8.7	7.0 - 8.12	9.9	1.50m
5' 0"	8.0	7.4 - 8.2	7.4 - 8.7	7.4 - 8.11	7.4 - 9.2	10.0	1.52m
5' 1"	8.3	7.7 - 8.5	7.7 - 8.10	7.7 - 9.1	7.7 - 9.7	10.5	1.55m
5' 2"	8.6	7.10 - 8.9	7.10 - 9.0	7.10 - 9.6	7.10 - 9.11	10.8	1.57m
5' 3"	8.9	7.13 - 8.13	7.13 - 9.4	7.13 - 9.10	7.13 - 10.2	10.13	1.60m
5' 4"	8.12	8.2 - 9.3	8.2 - 9.8	8.2 - 10.0	8.2 - 10.6	11.4	1.63m
5' 5"	9.2	8.6 - 9.7	8.6 - 9.13	8.6 - 10.5	8.6 - 10.10	11.9	1.65m
5' 6"	9.6	8.10 - 9.11	8.10 - 10.3	8.10 - 10.10	8.10 - 11.1	12.0	1.68m
5' 7"	9.10	9.0 - 10.1	9.0 - 10.7	9.0 - 11.1	9.0 - 11.6	12.5	1.70m
5' 8"	10.0	9.4 - 10.5	9.4 - 10.12	9.4 - 11.6	9.4 - 11.11	12.10	1.73m
5' 9"	10.4	9.8 - 10.9	9.8 - 11.2	9.8 - 11.10	9.8 - 12.2	13.1	1.75m
5' 10"	10.8	9.12 - 11.0	9.12 - 11.7	9.12 - 12.0	9.12 - 12.6	13.7	1.78m
5' 11"	10.12	10.2 - 11.4	10.2 - 11.12	10.2 - 12.5	10.2 - 12.12	13.13	1.80m
6' 0"	11.2	10.6 - 11.9	10.6 - 12.3	10.6 - 12.9	10.6 - 13.2	14.5	1.83m
6' 1"	11.6	10.10 - 12.0	10.10 - 12.8	10.10 - 13.0	10.10 - 13.7	14.11	1.85m
6' 2"	11.10	11.0 - 12.4	11.0 - 12.12	11.0 - 13.5	11.0 - 13.13	15.3	1.88m

Exercise is the Key

The benefits of exercise are incontrovertible: it keeps your cardiovascular system tip-top, and strengthens your bones and joints. Both are essential to enjoying life to the full. Aerobic exercise, like walking, cycling and swimming, increases the metabolic rate, and this helps us burn off calories. The goal is to work out at 60 to 75 per cent of your maximum heart rate, which gets you to that fat-burning level of activity. Your doctor will tell you what that level should be for you.

The good news is that you don't need to be a natural athlete to get the benefits. Even moderate doses of activity boosts the metabolism. Move enough every day and you raise your resting metabolic rate so that you can still work off calories and fat when you aren't exercising.

Research shows that people who lost weight and built exercise into their lives – i.e. committed themselves to a major change of lifestyle – kept the weight off. Such success requires discipline, because you need a fixed routine for exercise to work. Something as simple as skipping three times a week along with two to three brisk walks is all it takes to help you maintain your weight and fitness. Discipline in exercise, i.e. building it into your diary and committing to it (as you do other important things in your life), reinforces discipline in eating habits.

I know what you are thinking. You are telling yourself that you are already very active, rushing around and doing this or that. You get plenty of 'exercise', but still don't feel fit, and would like to worry less about putting on weight. Indeed, we all suffer from delusions about the amount we exercise. In 1991, Allied Dunbar carried out the largest ever fitness survey in the United Kingdom. A confident 80 per cent of the British said that they considered themselves 'fit', yet less than one-third of the men and two-thirds of the women could walk for several minutes up a gentle slope without becoming breathless. Hence, just dashing about and getting through the rough and tumble of everyday life does not make us fit. What *does* are certain activities that raise the heart-rate for a sustained period (at least twenty minutes four times a week), increase our stamina and work our muscles.

The very idea of exercise leaves many women weak. The best intentions to get fit and switch to a healthier diet somehow never manage to hold for more than the first few weeks after Christmas or just before that summer holiday. To become fit, especially if you have been relatively unfit for years, requires you to be creative about what will motivate you to become and stay active. Maybe it will take a strident personal trainer, in whom you might need to invest a percentage of your take-home income, to get you out of bed in the morning and put you through your paces. Or, perhaps it means getting a mate to join a badminton club with you. Many older women who rediscover dancing report that the inches just seem to 'fall off' when they keep it up regularly. If swimming is about the only thing you can face, be sure to go with friends to minimise any embarrassment you might feel in learning your way around the leisure centre for the first few weeks. Whatever it takes, do it – make that commitment.

Consult the Experts

Before you move a muscle, consult the experts and get a personal assessment of your current level of fitness, your nutritional status, a medical profile, your lifestyle and your personal goals for feeling and looking better. You will want a combination of advice from your doctor and a personal fitness adviser. The latter may be available for free or for a nominal fee at the local leisure centre, or you can hire a personal trainer by contacting the National Register of Personal Trainers (see Resource Directory at the end).

KEEPING STRESS UNDER CONTROL

1. Exercise will make you stay calmer. It reduces your adrenaline, and boosts the production of endorphins, 'Nature's morphine'.

2. Feed your body nutritional fuel every two to four hours. Low blood sugar makes you feel depressed.

3. Alleviate stress by taking B complex vitamins, Vitamin C, zinc, calcium, magnesium and ginseng (but avoid the latter if you have high blood pressure).

4. To keep cool, cut the caffeine in your life. You know about coffee and tea, but watch the 'blind caffeine' pervasive in many soft drinks.

5. Get enough sleep, and prepare yourself for shutdown: have regular baths before bed; refuse to be drawn into arguments after dinner; read only enjoyable things – not work! – before retiring.

6. Watch the alcohol intake. This encourages overeating and can make you irritable before bed, causing unsettled sleep, not to mention a lousy head in the morning.

7. Give yourself something to look forward to. Plan a holiday, or take a course in something you love. If we can't look ahead with enthusiasm today's hassles will seem more important than they need to be. Besides, you deserve a break.

Conclusion

It has been a joy to plan, research and write this book. Not only have I been able to share solutions to problems that have bothered so many of my clients over the years, but through my research I have discovered the existence of so many new resources available for the big and beautiful. The retailers are tripping over themselves to give you what you want – fashions like everyone else, only designed to suit *you*. No-one expects you to feel guilty any longer about not corresponding to some unrealistic notion of size and beauty. The days of aspiring to look like an adolescent stick-insect are over.

Real women come in every shape, size, colouring and personality. I hope that after reading this book, you will have dismissed some of your inclinations to hide your body, and yourself. You will have learned how special your colouring is, and what to wear from now on to look healthier and more attractive. Your 'black only' days should now be a thing of the past. Rather than worry any longer about the size labels inside your clothes, you now plan to go for the cut and the style, so that your clothes suit your shape. You no longer give a toss about a meaningless size.

You know you are worth time and investment – whatever your lifestyle and budget allows. You are going to indulge more in pampering yourself, having made a list of priorities after reviewing all the possibilities. Will it be a whole-body massage or a manicure this month? Is it time to get a gang together for a Lambada evening or a badminton tournament? And isn't it time you had your make-up done by an expert to learn some new techniques or switched hairdressers to someone more interested in *you*?

Whatever's got you excited about developing your image, so that the world appreciates you even more, go for it! A more confident, happy and stylish woman is waiting to be unveiled. And I'm cheering her on.

COSMETIC SURGERY: GIMMICK OR GODSEND?

Mention the notion of cosmetic surgery as a solution to deal with excess fat, and you open a Pandora's box of opinions. These range from the right-on 'fat is beautiful' brigade, who insist that fat in every form is glorious, to the psychologically unstable who believe that surgery is the answer to all life's problems. I have to take my hat off to the actress Roseanne Barr who, obese for years, had liposuction to remove excess fat then committed herself to a total change of lifestyle, eating more healthily and exercising for the first time in her life. Roseanne will never be svelte, nor is she madly pursuing the unattainable. She'll always be a grand size, but what a glamorous grand gal she is today.

After researching the possibilities of cosmetic surgery, I come out in favour of certain procedures as possible options for women with the money and the inclination to seek a permanent alternative to a lifelong hassle.

Liposuction or Liposculpture

Available for over ten years, liposuction has become one of the most popular cosmetic surgery procedures. There are two names for the same technique, but the former more honestly describes the procedure, while the latter makes the idea of having fat vacuumed off your body sound more aesthetic. Areas of unwanted fat are eliminated with a blunt-tip instrument called a cannula which moves beneath the skin, breaking up and moving fat cells. An operation can take from as little as 30 minutes up to two hours depending on the extent of the work necessary.

The operation is straightforward enough but patients need to prepare themselves for the after-effects – bruising, swelling, soreness and numbness. You have to wear an elasticated support garment for six to eight weeks, and the results aren't evident until about a month after the recovery.

Liposuction is recommended and used to remove the kind of stubborn fat accumulation, like cellulite, which has proved impossible to effect either through a change of eating habits or exercise.

The Risks of Liposuction

The horror stories of women ending up more disfigured after liposuction than before should be a thing of the past, provided that the surgeon you select is using the latest equipment and techniques which should produce minimal scarring.

Although considered safe, there are always risks, as with any surgical procedure. Blood and fat clots, infections and even death can occur, although these are rare. The occasional job can be botched, with the skin surface ending up rippled, or there is an imbalanced or asymmetrical result, such as two thighs different sizes. To minimise risks, you need to be referred to a good surgeon and to be healthy yourself with fairly resilient skin.

Liposuction should not be pursued without a

complementary plan to eat and exercise sensibly. Top London cosmetic surgeon Jan Stanek advises that 'Liposuction requires an agreement between doctor and patient to use the surgical procedure in parallel with a change of lifestyle. The best long-term results come from eating better and not returning to a sedentary life after surgery'.

Leg Reshaping

Shapeless legs can plague a woman regardless of her size. Here's another feature you can blame on the genes! But restricting yourself to dark, opaque tights and long skirts for life might not be necessary any longer. Again, liposuction can be used to remove excess fat around the knees and ankles to give you legs you'd be proud to show off. The procedure has no scarring.

Breast Reduction

Women with large, pendulous breasts that cause normal activities to be restricted, can consider breast-reduction surgery. You and the surgeon decide what size decrease would be right for you. Under general anaesthetic, the nipple is removed and an incision is made vertically and continued underneath the breast. Excess skin and breast tissue are removed by cutting, and the nipple is then replaced. Scarring will result from the incision marks but these will fade within four to six months.

It is recommended that breast reduction should be considered only after child-bearing, as pregnancy can risk stretching the scar tissue.

Selecting a Cosmetic Surgeon

Every country has its associations of plastic and cosmetic surgeons with lists of members. Such lists, however, are not a guarantee of finding a surgeon with the latest skills, the right kind of experience, and at the best price. So, it is up to you to do your homework about any surgeon or clinic before signing up. The horror stories of women who've been disfigured by cosmetic surgery are too many to enumerate, and should be salutary lessons to us all.

What to Ask of Your Cosmetic Surgeon

- Verifiable credentials. Check with any listed affiliation to ensure that s/he is truly a member.

- Explanation of recent/updated training. All top surgeons should regularly attend conferences and trainings on the latest techniques.

- The names and contact numbers of former patients. Don't be swayed only by their convincing 'before' and 'after' pictures. If you can, arrange to meet a former, satisfied patient, and see the results for yourself.

- You should also approach other cosmetic surgeons for alternative opinions. This should not be colleagues in the same clinic but other surgeons operating independently. Each visit will be charged, but the investment will be well worth if it you escape being operated on by one of the many 'cowboy' doctors able to circumvent registration law and recognised trading practices.

COLOUR APPENDIX

THE WARM TYPES: CMB Warm Spring or Warm Autumn

Golden tones will be your best but consider all the other colourful possibilities in your palette. Warm Springs have a brighter look (sparkling eyes) than Warm Autumns (deeper eyes).

Warm Spring Palette
 1 Camel
 2 Khaki
 3 Bronze
 4 Golden brown
 5 Dark brown
 6 Gold
 7 Ivory
 8 Cream
 9 Stone
10 Taupe
11 Grey green
12 Medium grey
13 Light peach
14 Peach
15 Deep peach
16 Light orange
17 Clear salmon
18 Coral
19 Mango
20 Tomato red
21 Terracotta
22 Marigold
23 Pumpkin
24 Rust
25 Buttermilk
26 Buff
27 Light clear gold
28 Bright golden yellow
29 Yellow gold
30 Bright yellow green
31 Mint
32 Pastel yellow green

33 Light true green
34 Lime
35 Light moss
36 Moss
37 Light aqua
38 Clear aqua
39 Light teal
40 Turquoise
41 Emerald turquoise
42 Jade
43 Medium blue
44 Deep periwinkle
45 Violet
46 Purple
47 Light navy
48 Teal

Warm Autumn Palette
 1 Camel
 2 Khaki
 3 Grey green
 4 Golden brown
 5 Coffee brown
 6 Dark brown
 7 Ivory
 8 Cream
 9 Stone
10 Taupe
11 Pewter
12 Medium grey
13 Light peach
14 Deep peach
15 Salmon

16 Salmon pink
17 Coral
18 Pumpkin
19 Terracotta
20 Tomato red
21 Bittersweet
22 Rust
23 Mahogany
24 Aubergine
25 Buttermilk
26 Buff
27 Light clear gold
28 Yellow gold
29 Light moss
30 Lime
31 Moss
32 Olive
33 Bronze
34 Mustard
35 Marigold
36 Gold
37 Turquoise
38 Emerald turquoise
39 Jade
40 Teal
41 Forest green
42 Light true green
43 Clear aqua
44 Light aqua
45 Violet
46 Deep periwinkle
47 Purple
48 Light navy

THE DEEP TYPES: CMB Deep Autumn or Deep Winter

Rich, strong and bold colours are your most complimentary. Deep Autumns have warmer skintone and hair colour while Deep Winters have more olive, neutral beige or porcelain skin. Dark skintones should compare which palette is best on their skin.

Deep Autumn Palette

1 Taupe
2 Pewter
3 Grey green
4 Black brown
5 Charcoal
6 Black
7 Soft white
8 Ivory
9 Cream
10 Stone
11 Camel
12 Buttermilk
13 Light peach
14 Deep peach
15 Salmon pink
16 Mango
17 Bittersweet
18 Tomato red
19 True red
20 Terracotta
21 Rust
22 Mahogany
23 Brown burgundy
24 Aubergine
25 Yellow gold
26 Marigold
27 Mustard
28 Light moss
29 Moss
30 Gold
31 Lime
32 Olive
33 Bronze
34 True green
35 Emerald green
36 Forest green
37 Mint
38 Hot turquoise
39 Chinese blue
40 Turquoise
41 Emerald turquois
42 Pine
43 True blue
44 Teal
45 Navy
46 Purple
47 Deep periwinkle
48 Silver

Deep Autumn Palette

1 Taupe
2 Pewter
3 Grey green
4 Black brown
5 Charcoal
6 Black
7 Soft white
8 Ivory
9 Cream
10 Stone
11 Camel
12 Buttermilk
13 Light peach
14 Deep peach
15 Salmon pink
16 Mango
17 Bittersweet
18 Tomato red
19 True red
20 Terracotta
21 Rust
22 Mahogany
23 Brown burgundy
24 Aubergine
25 Yellow gold
26 Marigold
27 Mustard
28 Light moss
29 Moss
30 Gold
31 Lime
32 Olive
33 Bronze
34 True green
35 Emerald green
36 Forest green
37 Mint
38 Hot turquoise
39 Chinese blue
40 Turquoise
41 Emerald turquois
42 Pine
43 True blue
44 Teal
45 Navy
46 Purple
47 Deep periwinkle
48 Silver

THE LIGHT TYPES: CMB Light Spring or Light Summer

Colourful tones that don't 'shout' along with pastels and elegant neutrals are your best. Light Springs have warmer skintone (ivory, possibly a few freckles), while Light Summers are cooler in skintone (pinker base or beige).

Light Spring Palette

1 Camel
2 Khaki
3 Pewter
4 Light grey
5 Medium grey
6 Blue charcoal
7 Soft white
8 Ivory
9 Stone
10 Taupe
11 Light peach
12 Warm pastel pink
13 Powder pink
14 Peach
15 Clear salmon
16 Coral
17 Light orange
18 Mango
19 Rose pink
20 Coral pink
21 Warm pink
22 Deep rose
23 Watermelon
24 Clear red
25 Buttermilk
26 Buff
27 Light clear gold
28 Bright golden yellow
29 Pastel yellow green
30 Light moss
31 Bright yellow green
32 Blue green
33 Emerald turquoise
34 Light teal
35 Clear aqua

36 Light aqua
37 Mint
38 Powder blue
39 Light lavender
40 Sky blue
41 Periwinkle
42 Purple
43 Violet
44 Light navy
45 True blue
46 Medium blue
47 Silver
48 Gold

Light Summer Palette
1 Light grey
2 Grey blue
3 Medium grey
4 Pewter
5 Cocoa
6 Rose brown

7 Soft white
8 Ivory
9 Rose beige
10 Stone
11 Taupe
12 Gold
13 Warm pastel pink
14 Powder pink
15 Clear salmon
16 Rose pink
17 Rose
18 Silver
19 Coral pink
20 Warm pink
21 Mango
22 Deep rose
23 Watermelon
24 Clear red
25 Buttermilk
26 Light lemon yellow
27 Mint
28 Pastel blue green

29 Light aqua
30 Clear aqua
31 Blue green
32 Emerald turquoise
33 Light teal
34 Soft teal
35 Spruce
36 Light navy
37 Lavender
38 Powder blue
39 Sky blue
40 Medium blue
41 True blue
42 Cadet blue
43 Lavender
44 Amethyst
45 Periwinkle
46 Deep periwinkle
47 Violet
48 Purple

THE SOFT TYPES: CMB Soft Summer or Soft Autumn

Best in muted not bold colours. Soft Summers have cooler skintone (pink or beige), with Soft Autumns definitely warmer (peachy, warm beige or even a few freckles)

Soft Summer Palette
1 Light grey
2 Medium grey
3 Grey green
4 Pewter
5 Coffee brown
6 Rose brown
7 Soft white
8 Ivory
9 Rose beige
10 Stone
11 Taupe
12 Cocoa
13 Powder pink
14 Dusty rose
15 Orchid
16 Rose pink
17 Rose
18 Soft fuchsia
19 Raspberry
20 Warm pink
21 Deep rose
22 Watermelon
23 Blue red
24 Burgundy

25 Buttermilk
26 Light lemon yellow
27 Mint
28 Pastel blue green
29 Blue green
30 Emerald turquoise
31 Turquoise
32 Jade
33 Spruce
34 Forest green
35 Soft teal
36 Teal
37 Light navy
38 Grey blue
39 Charcoal
40 Cadet blue
41 Sky blue
42 Periwinkle
43 Deep periwinkle
44 Amethyst
45 Purple
46 Medium blue
47 Silver
48 Gold

Soft Autumn Palette
1 Mahogany
2 Dark brown
3 Rose brown
4 Coffee brown
5 Grey green
6 Charcoal
7 Taupe
8 Cream
9 Camel
10 Khaki
11 Pewter
12 Medium grey
13 Light peach
14 Warm pink
15 Deep rose
16 Salmon
17 Silver
18 Gold
19 Salmon pink
20 Bittersweet
21 Tomato red
22 Watermelon
23 Rust
24 Terracotta

25 Soft white
26 Ivory
27 Stone
28 Buttermilk
29 Buff
30 Light lemon yellow
31 Yellow gold
32 Mint

33 Emerald turquoise
34 Turquoise
35 Jade
36 Teal
37 Bronze
38 Moss
39 Light moss
40 Lime

41 Olive
42 Forest green
43 Cadet blue
44 Light navy
45 Deep periwinkle
46 Amethyst
47 Purple
48 Aubergine

THE CLEAR TYPES: CMB Clear Spring or Clear Winter

Bright colours worn alone or in contrast. Clear Springs have warmer skintone, while Clear Winters are cooler or more neutral in skintone.

Clear Spring Palette

1 Navy
2 Light grey
3 Medium grey
4 Charcoal
5 Black
6 Black brown
7 Soft white
8 Ivory
9 Stone
10 Taupe
11 Pewter
12 Silver
13 Icy blue
14 Icy violet
15 Warm pastel pink
16 Clear salmon
17 Coral
18 Coral pink
19 Warm pink
20 Mango
21 Deep rose
22 Hot pink
23 Clear red
24 True red
25 Light clear gold
26 Lemon yellow
27 Bright golden yellow
28 Mint
29 Pastel yellow greene
30 Gold
31 Emerald turquoise
32 Kelly green
33 True green

34 Emerald green
35 Forest green
36 Olive
37 Light teal
38 Clear teal
39 Chinese blue
40 Clear aqua
41 Hot turquoise
42 Violet
43 Purple
44 Periwinkle
45 Deep periwinkle
46 Medium blue
47 Royal blue
48 Navy

Clear Winter Palette

1 Light grey
2 Medium grey
3 Charcoal
4 Black
5 Black brown
6 Pewter
7 Pure white
8 Soft white
9 Icy yellow
10 Icy grey
11 Stone
12 Taupe
13 Icy blue
14 Icy violet
15 Icy pink
16 Shocking pink

17 Hot pink
18 Deep rose
19 Mango
20 Clear red
21 Blue red
22 True red
23 Raspberry
24 Silver
25 Fuchsia
26 Magenta
27 Cranberry
28 Burgundy
29 Aubergine
30 Gold
31 Mint
32 Lemon yellow
33 Bright golden yellow
34 Hot turquoise
35 Chinese blue
36 Clear teal
37 Emerald turquoise
38 True green
39 Emerald green
40 Pine
41 Periwinkle
42 Violet
43 Bright periwinkle
44 Purple
45 True blue
46 Medium blue
47 Royal blue
48 Navy

THE COOL TYPES: CMB Cool Summer or Cool Winter

Colours that are both soft and rich will be your best, provided that you steer clear of golden tones. Cool Summers need softer colours, while Cool Winters can wear bolder, cool tones.

Cool Winter Palette

1 Icy grey
2 Light grey
3 Medium grey
4 Charcoal
5 Black
6 Black brown
7 Pure white
8 Soft white
9 Stone
10 Taupe
11 Pewter
12 Silver
13 Dusty rose
14 Rose pink
15 Shocking pink
16 Hot pink
17 Fuchsia
18 Magenta
19 Deep rose
20 True red
21 Blue red
22 Raspberry
23 Cranberry
24 Burgundy
25 Mint
26 Icy green
27 Icy yellow
28 Icy blue
29 Icy violet
30 Icy pink
31 Lemon yellow
32 Blue green
33 Emerald turquoise

34 True green
35 Emerald green
36 Pine
37 Hot turquoise
38 Chinese blue
39 Clear teal
40 Teal
41 Medium blue
42 Deep periwinkle
43 Bright periwinkle
44 True blue
45 Royal blue
46 Navy
47 Purple
48 Plum

Cool Summer Palette

1 Light grey
2 Medium grey
3 Blue charcoal
4 Grey blue
5 Charcoal
6 Pewter
7 Soft white
8 Rose beige
9 Stone
10 Taupe
11 Cocoa
12 Rose brown
13 Icy pink
14 Dusty rose
15 Rose pink
16 Orchid

17 Hot pink
18 Soft fuchsia
19 Deep rose
20 True red
21 Blue red
22 Watermelon
23 Raspberry
24 Burgundy
25 Light true green
26 Emerald turquoise
27 Teal
28 Soft teal
29 Spruce
30 Pine
31 Light lemon yellow
32 Mint
33 Medium aqua
34 Clear aqua
35 Hot turquoise
36 Chinese blue
37 Sky blue
38 Lavender
39 Amethyst
40 Violet
41 Plum
42 Purple
43 Periwinkle
44 Cadet blue
45 True blue
46 Royal blue
47 Navy
48 Silver

RESOURCE DIRECTORY

International Labels

All these labels cater for size 16 (12/14 USA and Canada) and up.

Godske (Denmark)
Finn Karelia (Finland)
The L Collection/L-Kolttu OY
    (Finland)
Viki by Pola (Finland)
Givenchy en Plus (France)
Rodier (France)
Virginie (France)
Weinberg (France)
Antonette (Germany)
Cartoon Two (Germany)
Claudia Moden (Germany)
Goldix (Germany)

Kohlhaas (Germany)
Laundry by Shelli Segal (Germany)
Patrizia by Mondi (Germany)
Schneberger (Germany)
Willie (Germany)
Condici (Italy)
Glaser and Gibi (Italy)
Liola (Italy)
Lucia (Italy)
Marina Rinaldi (Italy)
Almia (Sweden)
Big is Beautiful at Hennes (Sweden)
Adrianna Papell (US)

Cattiva (US)
Cherokee (US)
Counterparts II
Elisabeth by Liz Claibourne (US)
Ellen Tracy (US)
Forgotten Woman (US)
George Simonton (US)
JH Collectibles (US)
Jones of New York (US)
Lane Bryant (US)
Lesley Fay (US)
Outlander (US)
Venezia (US)

UK Resources

Labels
Ann Harvey   01582 23131
AS at Richards   0181 910 1208
Betty Barclay   0171 580 3577
BHS   0171 262 3288
Big is Beautiful at Hennes   0171 323 2211
Elvi   0121 236 9061
Evans   0171 636 8040
Jacques Vert Plus   0171 377 1900
Jean Muir   0171 831 0691
Ken Smith Designs   0171 631 3341
Luna   0151 3277176
Marks & Spencer   0171 935 4422
Nicole Farhi   0171 287 8787
Norman Linton   0171 267 0921
One   01455 238137
Rogers & Rogers   0171 706 7605
Selfridges   0171 629 1234
1647   0171 722 1647
Tricoville   0171 580 7137
Viki by Pola   015532 795556

Little But Large Labels
Eastex   0171 580 7866
Evans   0171 636 8040
Gabriella Rossi from Jacques Vert Plus   0171 377 1597

UK Mail Order for Larger Sizes
Ann Summers   0181 763 0122
Anna Hillman   01242 578758
The Classic Combination   0161 2369911
Flamedragon Belts   01603 714378
Fuller Taller   0121 523 2326
Katerine Wells   01303 863439
Littlewoods   0151 949 1111
Long Tall Sally   0181 689 9000
1647   0171 722 1647
Variations by Freemans   0800 900 200
Wetherall   01745 815592
XTRA Fashions   0117 9678650

Lingerie & Underwear
Ballet   00 3531 309663
Berlei   0525 850088
Bravissimo   01865 310123
Delia Marketing   0181 965 8707
Playtex   01483 291450
Triumph   01483 291450
Warners   01602 795796

Swimwear
Triumph International   01793 722200

Shoes

British Footwear Manufacturers Association
0171 734 8901
Medissa Shoes   0113 2530369
Small & Tall Shoe Shop   0171 723 5321

Miscellaneous

Diet Breakers 01869 37070
National anti-diet campaign. You count,
calories don't. Workshops & training for a healthy
lifestyle.

National Register of Personal Fitness Trainers 0181 944
6688

The Society of Teachers of the Alexander Technique
0171 351 0828

Surgical Advisory Service 0171 637 3110

Weight Watchers 01628 777077

New Zealand Resources

Manufacturers, Outlets and Labels

Extremes
Shop: The Mall, Northcote, Auckland   Ph: 09 419 1744
Labels: Kiss, Sunflower (Kiss Manufacturing)

Flexible Fashions
Shop: 602 Mt Albert Road, Royal Oak, Auckland
Ph: 09 625 7292
Labels: John Casuals, Enid II, Jean de Courey, 5PM,
Sycamore, Breeze

The Carpenter's Daughter:
Shops: Newmarket   Ph: 09 520 6646,
Takapuna   Ph: 09 488 0997,
Mt Albert, Auckland   Ph: 09 624 1715
Labels: Cashews, InHouse, Platform

Precious Vessells
Shops: 559 Manukau Rd, Greenwoods Corner, Epsom
Ph: 603 5885
555 Manukau Rd, Greenwoods Corner, Epsom
(Lingerie)
Labels: Precious Vessells, Anna Fitzpatrick, Initial,
Westlake, Sarah Jane, Staggers

Kooky Fashions
Shops: Takapuna, Newmarket, LynnMall (10 outlets
throughout NZ)   Ph: 09 489 6395
Label: Kooky Fashions
Dagmar Fashions
Auckland   Ph: 09 483 7472
Label: Dagmar

Rosemarie Muller Fashion Design
Shop: Rosemarie Muller, 279 Parnell Road, Parnell,
Auckland   Ph: 09 309 7848
Label: Rosemarie Muller

Courtenay
Auckland   Ph: 09 445 7332
Label: Top Drawer (Sleepwear and Lingerie)

Career Fashions Ltd.
Auckland   Ph: 09 366 0314
Label: Career Fashion

Cotura Fashions Lts.
Christchurch   Ph: 03 366 6958
Labels: Cotura, Hendricksen, Yokko

A Modo Mio Designer Fashions
Shop: 128 Willis Street, Wellington   Ph: 04 385 0020
Label: Chrissy Potter

Australian Resources

Anthea Crawford	Peer Gynt
ARC	Perri Cutten
BIB (Big Is Beautiful)	Robert D'Angelo
Big Apple	by Table Eight
Covers	Simona Plus
Dolin	Skirt Master
Elizabeth S	Susanne Blake
Evelyn Eve	Taking Shape
Maggie T	Think Big

Canadian Resources

Cotton Ginny Plus (sizes 14+)
Cotton Ginny Plus Intimates (sizes 14+ lingerie)
Toni Plus   Toll-free number 1-800-625-PLUS (7587),
across Canada, for mail order brochure

INDEX

Page numbers in *italic* refer to the illustrations

More from COLOR ME BEAUTIFUL

• Personal Image Classes

Color Me Beautiful have a comprehensive network of highly trained image consultants who offer individual and group consultations on colour, style and make-up. You can visit a consultant for a one-to-one session or bring a friend for a joint session. Each consultation includes a workbook and at our popular colour analysis session you receive an elegant wallet with 48 fabric swatches representing your best colours.

• Color Me Beautiful products

An exclusive range of cosmetics, skincare, scarves and fashion accessories are available from your local CMB consultant or direct via our mail-order catalogue.

• A Color Me Beautiful Career

If you enjoy helping people make the most of themselves, CMB can offer a challenging and rewarding career. Call or send for details and you will receive a free career pack on how to become a CMB Image Consultant. This flexible career can be run on a full or part-time basis, from a business premises or your home and can offer an exciting add-on service alongside an existing, compatible business.

• Business Seminars and Promotions

Entertaining and informative presentations and seminars are in demand by retailers as well as companies who recognise the importance of a good personal and company image. CMB have developed exciting joint promotions and valued incentives for clients who want loyal customers or staff to feel recognised and rewarded.

For further details on any of the above services/products, please complete and return the freepost information request form below. Alternatively, call us on 0171 627 5211

INFORMATION REQUEST FORM

Please send me information on the following:

CMB IMAGE CONSULTANTS

(tick the boxes as necessary)

Personal Image Classes ☐

CMB Products ☐

CMB Career ☐

Business Seminars ☐

NAME: _____ *(please print)*

ADDRESS: _____

_____

DAYTIME TELEPHONE NO: _____

PHOTO CREDITS

Please note that items of clothing not credited are the models' own.

page 10 clothes by 1647; *page 14* photographs by Richard Barnes for *Yes!* magazine; *page 23* illustration courtesy J D Williams; *page 28* photograph and clothes by Evans; *page 31* jacket by Jacques Vert Plus; *page 34* suit by Marina Rinaldi; *page 35* (left) clothes by Marks & Spencer, necklace by Adrien Mann; *page 37* photograph and clothes by Evans; *page 39* photographs and clothes by Evans; *page 45* photograph and clothes by Evans; *page 50* suit by Jacques Vert Plus; *page 52* ankle boots by Marks & Spencer; *page 54* all photographs and clothes by Evans; *page 61* clothes by Marks & Spencer; *page 66* photograph and clothes by Evans; *page 69* red jacket (3) by Jaeger; *page 77* trouser 1 by Liz Claiborne, trousers 2 and 3 by Marks & Spencer; *page 78* clothes by Marks & Spencer; *page 80* photograph courtesy Triumph International Limited; *pages 82, 87* and *88* underwear and photographs by Ann Summers; *page 89* swimsuit on left by Ann Summers, swimsuit on right by Evans; *page 92* photographs courtesy *My Weekly*; *page 95* photographs and clothes by Evans; *page 100* jacket and photograph by Elvi; *page 102* clothes and photograph by Jacques Vert Plus; *page 104* clothes by 1647; *pages 124-5* clothes and photographs by Evans; *page 126* (top) clothes and photographs by Evans; *page 126* (bottom), *127* and *128* clothes and photograph by 1647; *page 129* (top) clothes by Jaeger; *page 129* (bottom) clothes by Next; *page 152* photographs courtesy *My Weekly*; *page 157* photographs by Richard Barnes for *Yes!* magazine; *page 160* chart reproduced with permission of Weight Watchers (UK) Ltd.

Models for Evans photographs supplied by Ford Models (Mia Rosen and Maureen Roberts), and Hammond Hughes (Jackie Morgan)
Additional models supplied by Hammond Hughes and Excel

POSTAGE
PAID

CMB Image Consultants
FREEPOST
London SW8 3BR

a puzzled quarter of   to him and ran
thus

       "Please aw _____, ~~understand how~~
~~to act~~. Right wing three _____ _____ missing. indispensable
tomorrow. Overton"

       "Strand post mark and dispatched 9.36" said
Holmes, reading it over and over. "Mr Overton was evidently
considerably excited when he ~~dispatched~~ ^{sent} it and somewhat
incoherent in consequence. Well, well, he will be here I dare say ^{by}
the time I have looked through the Times
~~the time that the table is cleared~~ and then we shall know all about
it. Even the most insignificant problem would be welcome in these
stagnant times."

       Things had indeed been very slow with us, and I
had learned to dread such periods of inaction for I knew by
experience that my companion's brain was so abnormally active
that it was dangerous to leave it without material upon which to
work. For years I had gradually weaned him from that drug
mania which had threatened once to ~~destroy~~ ^{check} his remarkable
^{career} nature. Now I knew that under ordinary conditions he no longer
craved for this artificial stimulus but I was well aware that the
fiend was not dead but sleeping, and I have known that the
sleep was a light one and the waking near when in periods of
idleness I have seen the drawn look upon Holmes' ascetic face
and the brooding of his deep set and inscrutable eyes. Therefore
I blessed ^{this} Mr Overton, who ever he might be, since he had come
with his enigmatic message to break that dangerous calm which
brought more ^{peril} ~~danger~~ to my friend than all the storms of his
tempestuous life.